fool - 54+

Suffering - 86, 125, 158
— and Job - 96+, 106+, 110

Ten Commandments - 32

THE BOOK THAT IS ALIVE

BY JOHN PATERSON

The Goodly Fellowship of the Prophets
The Praises of Israel

THE BOOK
THAT IS ALIVE

Studies in Old Testament Life and Thought
as Set Forth by the Hebrew Sages

BY JOHN PATERSON

Professor of Hebrew and Old Testament Exegesis
Drew Theological Seminary, Madison, New Jersey

1954

CHARLES SCRIBNER'S SONS

New York

Acknowledgement is made to *Religion and Life* for permission to use the substance of two articles, *The Book That Is Alive* and *The Living Word,* which appeared in the Autumn 1946 and Spring 1948 issues. In this book they have been amplified and used in slightly altered form. Copyright 1946 and 1948.

Conjugi Dilectissimae

Contents

Foreword

THE PURPOSE OF THIS VOLUME is to set forth certain vital aspects of Hebrew Life and Thought. Inasmuch as the author has already published volumes on the Prophets of Israel and the Psalter the present work concerns itself mainly with the Wisdom Literature of the Old Testament. The writer has confined himself in what he has written to the canonical books as it was felt that to include Ecclesiasticus and the Wisdom of Solomon would raise problems far beyond the intended scope of this book. Occasional references have been made to Ecclesiasticus and relevant citations are introduced.

The first topic, from which the book takes its title, together with the second, were originally published in *Religion and Life* and appear here in slightly altered form. The author is much indebted to the Abingdon-Cokesbury Press for permission to use this material which appeared in Volume XV, No. 4, and Volume XVII, No. 2, of *Religion and Life*. The remainder of the volume consists of addresses given at Clergy Retreats and Adult Schools of Religion. This fact may account for certain homiletical suggestions that occur throughout the work.

In the citation of Scripture passages the Authorized Version has been used on the ground that this is the version most generally read and used in public worship. Frequently, the author has modified the text of this version to make it conform more closely to the Hebrew or Greek original. The numbering of the verses in citations is according to the English version.

The author desires to express his thanks to the Reverend Robert Markham, graduate student at Drew Theological Seminary and formerly assistant in the Old Testament department, for help in the preparation of the manuscript; to Dr. F. Heisse Johnson, now Dean of Administration at Tennessee Wesleyan College, Athens, Tennessee, and to Dr. Lawrence E. Toombs, his colleague in the Old Testament department, for counsel and suggestion.

John Paterson

DREW THEOLOGICAL SEMINARY
DREW UNIVERSITY
MADISON, NEW JERSEY
January 1954

THE BOOK THAT IS ALIVE

I

The Book That Is Alive

A MODERN POET records how once the doer of a heroic deed was unable to tell it to his fellow-tribesmen for lack of words.[1] Whereupon, continues the poet, there arose a man "afflicted with the necessary magic of words" and in terms so vivid and moving he told the story that his words "became alive and walked up and down in the hearts of his hearers." Whereupon, we are told, the tribesmen arose and put the inspired man to death. And the poet makes this comment on the tale:

> a bare half-hundred words, breathed upon by some man in his exaltation or his agony . . . generations ago, can open to us the doors of three worlds, or stir us so intolerably that we can scarce abide to look at our own souls. It is a miracle— one that happens very seldom.

We do not usually think of the Bible as the book that is alive and though we often sing of the "wonderful words of life" we have not really felt them walking up and down in our hearts or sensed their real vitality. The usual black binding of the Bible tends to convey an opposite impression, and one who seeks to show its quickening power labors under the disadvantage of a deep-rooted prejudice. Nonetheless, we are undertaking this task in the belief that it can be demonstated to reason and made perceptible to feeling and emo-

[1]Cited from James Alexander Robertson, *The Gospels and Epistles of St. John* (1919), p. 92.

1

tion. So often we fail to see the wood for the trees and even the trees may not be clear to our sight. But it is desirable that both the preacher and the teacher should get a comprehensive view and, like Moses on Pisgah's height, "see all the land." Later we can survey the individual features.

In our approach we must make one general premise. We will bear in mind that when we deal with the Bible we are dealing with an ancient literature whose methods of thought and expression differ greatly from our own. That is true particularly in the case of the Old Testament and it holds good also, though in lesser degree, with the New Testament. We are so accustomed to our own thought processes, derived mainly from Greek sources, that we forget that here we are concerned with a literature that knew little or nothing of such processes and all too frequently we make this book say what we think it should say and we fail to hear what it really does say. We stretch its ancient forms on our Procrustean molds until its beauty is marred, its vitality destroyed, and finally we see no beauty in it that we should desire it. Like Israel itself—to use a prophetic simile—it was once a noble vine but we have stripped it of its nobility and its glory has departed. It has become a barren withered thing. To recapture that nobility and show forth its native beauty is the purpose we have in view.

a) VITALITY OF THE WORD

To perceive and understand the vitality of Scripture, especially the Old Testament and the New Testament Gospels, we must begin with the matter of the spoken word. The Hebrew thought of this in a way that seems strange to us. The spoken word to the Hebrew was fearfully alive. It was not merely a vocable or sound dropped heedlessly from un-

thinking lips. It was *a unit of energy charged with power.*
It flies like a bullet to its billet. It is energized for weal or
woe. Words fall from our lips so easily and so idly. But the
Hebrew was economical of words: there was a marked austerity about his utterance. The Hebrew speech has less than
10,000 words while Greek has 200,000. Thus a word to the
Hebrew was something to be thought about and expended
carefully. It is significant that in Hebrew the word for
thought and speech is the same (*'amar*). Hebrew speech is
just thinking aloud—but it is thinking. Therefore, the characteristic prayer of the Hebrew was:

> Set a watch, O Lord, before my mouth;
> keep the door of my lips. (Psalm 141:3)

The Hebrew knew there was power in words and that such
power must not be used indiscriminately. Words "run" and
have "free course": they run to realize themselves. That may
seem somewhat primitive to us and naive but that idea still
prevails in the East. There when a curse is uttered the bystanders will throw themselves flat on the ground that those
words, like high explosives, may pass over their heads and
do them no harm. Sir George Adam Smith tells somewhere
how once as he journeyed in the desert a group of Moslems
gave his party the customary greeting, "Peace be upon you,"
and failed to notice that he, a Christian, was in the group.
When they learned that the Moslem greeting had thus been
extended to an infidel—for the Christian is an infidel to the
Moslem—they returned to ask back the greeting. A beneficent
force had been released where it should not be released and
they sought to recall it. We get something of that thought
in Will Carleton's verse:

> Boys flying kites haul in their white-winged birds;

You can't do that way when you're flying words:
"Careful with fire" is good advice, we know,
"Careful with words" is ten times doubly so.
Thoughts unexpressed may sometimes fall back dead,
But God himself can't kill them when they're said.[2]

The Hebrew went further than that. Words were dynamic and possessed inherent energy: they realized themselves. Neither Isaac nor Esau could recall the blessing given to Jacob, and for all their passionate tears the thing spoken was beyond recall (Genesis 27:1 f.). When the high priest spoke the Levitical blessing,

> The Lord bless thee and keep thee:
> The Lord make his face shine upon thee
>   and be gracious unto thee:
> The Lord lift up his countenance upon thee,
>   and give thee peace.   (Numbers 6:24–26)

the people not only heard words: they received to themselves a vital force that travelled with the words from the soul (*nephesh*) of the high priest to their souls. The blessing conveyed vitality.

Nor is all this at all fanciful. It is indeed far removed from our customary ways of thinking. Let us consider the curse and see how this worked. In Numbers 22 we are told of Balak and how he hired Balaam to lay a curse on Israel. Balak feared that his military force might not be sufficient to withstand the oncoming Israel but he knew something that would stop them—the curse. Balak knew that in procuring the services of Balaam he had acquired the most potent weapon of antiquity. A good curser or blesser was worth more than two army divisions. The curse was the thing! Anything after the curse could only be in the nature of "mopping up."

[2]Will Carleton, "The First Settler's Story" in *Farm Festivals*.

> Come now therefore, curse me this people; for they are too mighty for me: peradventure I shall prevail, that we may smite them, and that I may drive them out of the land: for I know that he whom thou blessest is blessed, and he whom thou cursest is cursed. (Numbers 22:6)

It would be no inexactitude to say that this was the way in which most of those ancient wars were won and lost. These were really battles of words in an unusual sense. Think of the story in I Kings 22 where we see Ahab and Jehoshaphat in all their embattled might ready to go forth to battle. But their campaign was doomed to failure despite the fawning words of the four hundred sycophantic prophets who prophesied success. The campaign was doomed to failure when the true word proceeded from the lips of Micaiah ben Yimla:

> And he said, I saw all Israel scattered upon the hills, as sheep that have not a shepherd: and the Lord said, These have no master: let them return every man to his house in peace. (I Kings 22:17)

That word runs and not all the king's horses or all the king's men can arrest its progress. The word is dynamic and vital. Shimei's curse, too, will run its course and David well knows there is nothing he can do about it (II Samuel 16:10 f.). Like the spot on the hand of Lady Macbeth nothing can wash it out. Not a word fails or falls to the ground: it cannot return void. Thus the divine word is, as Jeremiah says, "like a hammer that breaketh the rock in pieces" (Jeremiah 23:29). There is irresistible energy in it: it is fearfully alive.

b) VITALITY OF SEMITIC SPEECH

Hebrew speech differs considerably from ours. We may get used to the fact that it is read from right to left and that a Hebrew volume begins where ours ends. We can become accustomed to those rather strange features. But we cannot easily get used to the sounds of this speech: it abounds in sounds we can scarcely frame to express, deep guttural sounds that spring from deep down in the chest. Our own speech is largely a matter of the teeth and a sounding of the words against our ivories which produces a hissing, whistling sound. It is certainly not the most musical language. But when we cross to Italy and the sunny south we find there a language that is musical and a speech that is usually accompanied with much gesticulation and animated gesture. The whole body seems to speak and the speech flows from the *ore rotundo* and forms an ample utterance. But when we pass to the land of the Semites we find there a speech that is not centered in the teeth nor in the *ore rotundo* but is set deep down in the chest with all the power of the visceral and abdominal muscles behind it. That is a speech with all the blood and force of the heart behind it: it is essentially a language of the heart. It is a language of passion and it differs wholly from Latin deliberation and Greek moderation. It is significant that a Hebrew sentence usually begins with the verb, the word of action, while in a Latin sentence we must search long and far before we reach the verb at the end of the sentence. That represents the distinction between classical deliberation and Semitic energy and action for the Hebrew is interested primarily in action. The continuous use of lively interjections like "Lo," "Behold," and phrases like "See," "Consider," "Lift up your eyes" both in Old Testament and the Gospels suggest the extraordinary liveliness and vitality of the Hebrew speech.

c) VITALITY OF THOUGHT

Nor is it otherwise here. Language and thought combine

to give the living word. For the Hebrew is always concrete and definite. He is always in touch with life: there are no abstractions here. That holds likewise of the Gospel story though it does not hold with reference to Paul. The mind of the Hebrew was the intuitive mind. The speculative type is not found here save in the latest books of the Old Testament, mainly in Ecclesiastes where the pure Hebrew genius has been crossed with the Greek. Ecclesiastes does not reflect the native genius of the Semite, for normally the Hebrew saw only one thing at a time and he did not see things in their relations. So it is with Jesus: he sees the scarlet anemones that carpet the land, the fisherman's boat, the sower striding down the furrow as he scatters broadcast from his bosom, and the birds that circle overhead. The thought here is optical rather than logical, and of this we shall say more in a moment. But it enables us to understand why in the case of Socrates we get a system of philosophy while from Jesus we have words of life. Those words are not organized into a system but fall as words of beauty and grace from his lips while he sits by a well-side or hails a man up in a tree. Unstrung, these words lie like jewels in a casket and each separate jewel shines with its own beauty. The Hebrew knew it was impossible to "cordialize with an *ens rationis*" (rational entity) and he never made the attempt. He keeps his feet on the ground and grips reality: he gets down to "brass tacks" and speaks real things. The word here is always made flesh and he who runs may read: here are transcripts from life and slices of experience. Ideas get "a local habitation and a name" and become real before our eyes. "Ideas," says George Eliot, "are poor ghosts,

> our sun-filled eyes cannot discern them: they pass athwart us in their vapor, and cannot make themselves felt. But some-

times they are made flesh: they breathe upon us with warm breath, they touch us with soft responsive hands, they look at us with sad sincere eyes, and speak to us with appealing tones; they are clothed in a living human soul with all its conflicts, its faith, and its love. Then their presence is a power, then they shake us like a passion, and we are drawn after them with a gentle compulsion as flame is drawn to flame."[3]

In all noble literature it is so: the word is made flesh. The follies of youth are incarnated in the Prodigal Son and the abstract matter of charity and philanthropy becomes real in the story of the Good Samaritan. So these things come home to the bosoms and the business of men. That is why the Bible finds us in the deepest parts of our being. Deep calleth unto deep, and life speaks to the living.

We may attain this standard at times but we cannot maintain it. It is normal to the Hebrew. Their words smack of the soil: they reflect sensation with vivid directness. To the Hebrew, *anger* is "the fire that burns," *desire* is "the thirst that cannot be quenched," *pride* is the "the lofty look," *obstinacy* is "stiffness of neck." *Courage* is expressed by "girding the loins" or "strengthening the feeble knees," while *forgiveness* is "the blotting out" of transgressions. *Joy* is expressed by "dancing," *justice* is "the straight path," while *iniquity* is "the crooked way." Here men *think with the eye* and all comes in by the eye-gate.

Nor is it otherwise in the more spacious thoughts of life. We are used to speaking of the Problem of Suffering in the Old Testament, but the Bible does not know it so. Here the word becomes quivering flesh and we behold a Job sitting on his ash-heap outside the city gate or we discern dimly that wondrous form of the Suffering Servant (in Isaiah 53)

[3]George Eliot, *Scenes from Clerical Life,* n. d., p. 416.

whose beauty was marred beyond recognition. That is concrete and living. We speak again of temptation, but the
Bible takes us down to the house of Potiphar (Genesis 39)
and lets us see Joseph tempted and how in that hot hour
he keeps a hold on character as he keeps a hold on God and
says, "How can I do this great wickedness and sin against
God?" That surely is life as most of us have known it. Or
yet again the Bible takes us to Babylon and there it shows
us what fidelity means. It tells us of a young Jew who had
been carried captive there and who by his diligence had
attained to a position of high honor and responsibility. It
tells us how he held to the faith of his fathers and observed
the simple dietary laws as well as the major precepts of his
religion. It tells us how when he was threatened for his
faith and tempted to deny it he stood firm though a den of
lions waited to receive him (Daniel 6). The writer here
wanted to show the real nature of a godly Jew and how such
a Jew will be faithful to his God when tyrants like Nebu-
cadrezzar or Hitler or Mussolini seek to seduce them from
the faith of their fathers. He knew such times and such
tyrants would recur in history and he bodied forth this ideal
for the guidance of men. And so both Jew and Gentile look
at this and say to their children:

> Dare to be a Daniel,
> Dare to stand alone,
> Dare to have a purpose firm,
> Dare to make it known.

Fidelity is what we call that; the Jew was concrete and
vital, and he told the story of Daniel.

d) VITALITY OF MORAL INSIGHTS

We may pride ourselves as we will on our modern educational advances and our psychological techniques but has any teacher of religion ever given us an analysis of temptation equal to that found in Genesis 3? Could there be anything more vital than this presentation? It could easily be set forth in diagrammatic form as psychologists often do. All this comes in through the eye-gate. There is the woman who might have been busily employed but was not; she was caught off guard. "Satan finds some mischief for idle hands to do." And Satan finds some evil for empty minds to think. "A man's task is his life preserver," said Emerson, though he used it in a slightly different way. There, too, is the serpent, slimy, slithering, with all his sinuosity of coil insinuating himself into the garden, fascinating with his evil eye—where could we find a more apt picture of the insidiousness of temptation that worms its way into the citadel of Mansoul? Here we see temptation taking the form of *a*) a physical sensation, "good to eat," *b*) the form of an aesthetic delight "good to look upon," and finally *c*) the form of an intellectual ambition, "to be desired to make one wise."[4] This gets us on all sides. It is all so vivid and so vital. Thomas à Kempis tells us that the whole story of the Temptation and Fall may be put in four words. These, to quote his original Latin, are *Cogitatio, Imaginatio, Delectatio, Assensio.* The thought or cogitation may arise within ourselves or it may be due to external suggestion. Then we bring that thought from the periphery of consciousness into the center of the field of consciousness and form a picture or image (*imaginatio*) of it. We keep gazing upon it and our mouth waters with delight (*delectatio*) as it stands before our eyes. But that does not constitute the Fall of man: that results when something within us assents (*assensio*) to the suggestion and the citadel

[4]John Edgar MacFadyen, *The Use of the Old Testament* (1922), p. 30.

of Mansoul is laid in ruins. Assuredly the writer who painted
that picture and penned that story knew life and the work-
ings of the human heart. Here we have a slice from life as
it is lived, a veritable transcript from experience. This is
thinking with the eye.

So often we miss the vital message because we fail to
think thus with the eye. The reporter will get the words but
the camera gets the picture. The accompanying gestures are
never caught by the reporter, but it is the gestures and the
accompanying attitudes that are significant.

When the Psalmist says, "There are the workers of iniquity
fallen" (Psalm 36:12), we have to think of him pointing the
finger with triumphant joy at wicked men overthrown. When
Jesus spoke to the Syro-Phoenician woman, how did he look?
There must have been encouragement and challenge in his
look that led that woman to come back with that spirited
rejoinder:

> Yea, Lord: but even the little dogs eat of the crumbs that
> fall from their master's table.   (Matthew 15:27)

And as surely Jesus must have smiled broadly as he an-
swered:

> O woman, great is thy faith: be it unto thee even as thou
> wilt.   (Matthew 15:28)

How did Jesus look when "he looked round about on them
with anger" (Mark 3:5) and how did he appear when "Jesus
beholding him loved him" (Mark 10:21)? Or what did the
writer imply as to the Savior's look when he wrote, "He
began to be greatly amazed and sore troubled" (Mark 14:
33). Words only express so much and so much is left to
imagine. Nothing is so much to be desired in preacher or
teacher as the gift of sanctified imagination. So often the

commentaries on Scripture afford little help for they seek to set things in logical order. Here it is required that we should look rather for an optical connection and ask what was the speaker looking at and what did he see next. He had a roving eye and there was much to see; he was interested in life and the changing scene and the processes of the logical mind were a sealed book to him.

e) VITALITY IN POPULAR SAYINGS

We may seem to be laboring the present point but it is difficult to get inside the skin of the Semite; we are making the attempt from various sides. The attempt must be made if we are to understand what the Bible is saying to us. We are so used to abstractions that we fail to see we are often merely covering the obscurity of our thought with ambiguous terms and phrases and throwing dust in our own eyes. We lose contact with reality: the Hebrew always had his feet on the ground.

The present writer has heard a preacher begin his prayer with the words, "O Thou who art our great working hypothesis . . ." but he has never felt God was as far away as all that. These words could not be turned into Hebrew and prayers that cannot be put into Hebrew should not be prayed. Listen to the Hebrew as he communed with his God:

> O Lord, my strength, my rock, my fortress, my buckler, my
> lofty tower.   (Psalm 18:1–2)

A child could understand that and repeat it but an advanced Christian might not feel his heart awakened by that other artificial high-sounding phrase. "Create within me a clean heart, O Lord," or "God be merciful to me a sinner" can be said in Hebrew and are fit prayers for Everyman, for that is how a child speaks to his father.

Today we speak much of environment and heredity and often it is doubtful if we know what we really mean. The Hebrew knew what was involved there and he expressed it in a phrase that makes the spine tingle:

> The fathers have eaten sour grapes, and the children's teeth are set on edge.   (Ezekiel 18:2)

The Bible knows "the world, the flesh, and the devil" and there is no reason why we should gloze over these definite realities with our high-sounding phrases. We have seen a preacher advertised to preach on the "Immutability of Character" but the hearers might not guess easily what he was after. The ancient Semite, however, would have vitalized that topic for them with:

> Can the Ethiopian change his skin, or the leopard his spots?
>   (Jeremiah 13:23)

And could any phrase of ours express more adequately the dream that today is in the heart of every decent man:

> They shall beat their swords to plowshares and their spears to pruninghooks.   (Isaiah 2:4; Micah 4:3)

We pride ourselves on our ability to give expression to our thoughts and to create literary media. But we cannot equal the Hebrew in that respect. We call a spade an agricultural implement, but he called a spade a spade. Look at this same thing in Jewish and Arabic proverbs, and those proverbs are the crystallization of the thought of many centuries. We say *union is strength* where both terms are abstract; the Semite says, *two dogs killed a lion*: that is realistic and related to real life. It is something he has seen and observed. *Familiarity breeds contempt* is thoroughly English and completely abstract but how eloquent is the Jewish rendering of the same thought:

The poor man hungers and knows it not.

So long has the poor man been in company with his empty stomach that he is unconscious of its ache! Arabic yields a most expressive word on a problem that vexes us all today —the problem of juvenile delinquency:

> If the father be onion, and the mother garlic,
> How can the child have a sweet perfume?

That is pungent and penetrating: it goes right to the center of the problem and even suggests a solution! The Arabic proverbs are rooted in the soil and smack of Mother Earth. The following would have been well understood by Uriah Heap: it commends humility:

> Low-lying ground drinks its own rain
> and that of its neighbors.

There is insight in this one on the tongue:

> The tongue is the dragoman (*interpreter*) of the heart.

Nor is there anyone who will deny the forceful vigor of the truth expressed in

> He who increases his flesh increases food for worms.

These may lack polish but they do not lack vitality. Compared to these the English maxims are

> As moonlight unto sunlight
> And as water unto wine.

f) VISUALIZED EMOTION

To such a degree is this way of thinking developed by the lively Semite that even emotion could be made visible to the eye. We can never understand the pathos and tragedy of Cain until we *see* it as the Hebrew saw it:

But unto Cain and his offering he had not respect. And Cain
was very wroth, and his countenance fell.
And the Lord said unto Cain, Why art thou wroth? and why
is thy countenance fallen?   (Genesis 4:5, 6)

"Cain was very wroth" may not convey very much in English translation: something more is required and that something more is given. When the writer indicates that Cain's
"face was fallen" he is visualizing emotion. We see those lips
that once were upturned in a smile now fallen downwards
into a deadly frown. We can almost hear it like the falling
of a cart of bricks. Frequently we speak of passing out of
a state of depression into a state of exaltation but the Hebrew
added life to that:

Thou hast turned for me my mourning into dancing.

So says the Psalmist (Psalm 30:11) and says so much more
than we do with our abstractions. Or think again—and lastly
—of this word:

In six days the Lord made heaven and earth, and on the
seventh he rested and was refreshed.   (Exodus 31:17)

Was refreshed does not adequately render what the Hebrew
writer said; better would it be, "he drew his breath," or if
we may put it so, without loss of reverence, "he took a
breather."

As to how the Hebrew dealt with the metaphysical attributes of God, the thought of eternity, omnipresence, omnipotence and omniscience the author would refer to what he
has written elsewhere.[5] These matters also the Hebrew was
able to compass and adequately express in real and vital
fashion.

[5]*The Praises of Israel,* 1950, pp. 159–161.

g) VITALITY OF THE NEW TESTAMENT

This matter can be pursued in the pages of the New Testament. Is it not precisely this vital reference that makes the Gospels so attractive? We can understand and sympathize with Peter as he rubs his eyes with a sense of bewilderment, which many a student shares, over the Epistles of Paul "in which are some things hard to be understood" (II Peter 3:16). No one feels that way about the Gospels: but in Paul we get those big jaw-breaking words like sanctification, reconciliation, justification, and adoption. In the Gospels we have stories written from life in the living Hebrew style, stories which a child could read and understand.

> A certain man had two sons; And the younger of them said to his father, Father, give me the portion of goods that falleth to me. And he divided unto them his living.
> And not many days after the younger son gathered all together, and took his journey into a far country, and there wasted his substance with riotous living.
> And when he had spent all, there arose a mighty famine in that land; and he began to be in want. And he went and joined himself to a citizen of that country; and he sent him into his fields to feed swine.
> And he would fain have filled his belly with the husks that the swine did eat; and no man gave unto him.
> And when he came to himself, he said, How many hired servants of my father's have bread enough and to spare, and I perish with hunger!
> I will arise and go to my father, and will say unto him, Father, I have sinned against heaven and before thee,
> And am no more worthy to be called thy son: make me as one of thy hired servants.   (Luke 15:11 ff.)

Almost every word in that simple recital is good Anglo-Saxon and the words smell of the soil from which they spring. They are rooted in the countryside and common life. The terms quoted above from Paul are all Latin words lifted straight from Rome. It is small wonder that when people heard Jesus speak their hearts were thrilled with joy and they said, "We never heard it in this fashion so before." Here is something unspeakably fresh and in that respect Jesus is Hebrew through and through. Paul could not speak so, though he boasted of one hundred per cent Hebraism (II Corinthians 11:22). Jesus is definite and concrete in all his preaching and teaching; "the kingdom of God is like" . . . this or that concrete thing. The sower striding down the furrow with his seed, the birds that circle overhead, the fisherman's boat that dances on the lake, and the men drawing their nets aboard—all this is here and more. Always he thinks with the eye: always the word is made flesh. Truth embodied in a tale enters in at lowly doors. "The common people heard him gladly." The old Doctors Dryasdust did not, could not speak that way. The shadows of Greece and the Western world fall across the pages of Paul but in Jesus we have the native Hebrew genius. Hebrew has no roots larger than three letters and Jesus is simple as that. He thinks *optically* while Paul reasons *logically*. In the Gospels we have vital religion while in the Epistles we have theology. That may be putting the contrast too strongly but there is a real difference and any reader can feel the difference. Jesus asserts while Paul argues and somehow we feel with Tennyson "there is no dew upon the grass after a windy night." We would not be unfair to Paul—but we love the dew on the grass.

h) LANGUAGE OF THE NEW TESTAMENT

This chapter has been long enough and we will bring it to a close with a brief word concerning the language in which the New Testament is written. This bears very closely on the vitality of Scripture. The New Testament is written in Greek but it is not the classical Greek of Thucydides or Demosthenes. It is far removed from these classical writers, and scholars have often marvelled that such precious words of life should be penned in Greek so apparently debased. Some scholars of an earlier age deemed it a form of Greek without parallel elsewhere and spoke of it as "the language of the Holy Ghost." One might have surmised that the divine spirit would express itself in proper linguistic form but evidently that thought did not enter the minds of the scholars. But precisely here we find one of the most wonderful romances of the Egyptian desert, for within the last century thousands of documents, called papyri, have been discovered in Egypt. These documents deal with all kinds of matters, consist of private and intimate letters as well as business documents, and they lay bare that whole ancient life. Their real significance, however, lies in the fact that they reveal a form of the Greek language which was in common use over a wide area of the Near East, and this is the language in which our New Testament was first written. It was the speech of common people and for that reason it is called *Koinē*, which is the Greek word for common. Thus the New Testament was written in the language of the common people and its literary form springs from the workaday life of plain folk. Thus again we observe how deeply the Bible is rooted in the life of men. It owes its vitality to its vital origins.

II

The Divine Library

When Sir Walter Scott lay dying at Abbotsford he turned to his son-in-law, J. G. Lockhart, who later became his biographer, and asked him to read to him. Lockhart asked what he would like to have read and Sir Walter replied, "Need you ask? there is but one book." Lockhart understood and took the Bible and read from the fourteenth chapter of John's Gospel. And "the wizard of the North," who has often been compared with the story-teller "J" of Genesis, was comforted with those words of life.

a) VARIED AS LIFE ITSELF

Let us leave this matter of story-telling for a moment and center on those words of Sir Walter: "there is but one book." And that book we know as the *Holy Bible*. But that Bible is really a library of books and this library consists of 66 separate books, 39 being in the Old Testament and 27 in the New Testament. Here are books by different authors, known and unknown, books of varying literary quality and widely divergent spiritual value. Law and Prophecy are here and the Writings (*Kethubim*), too, with their somewhat miscellaneous content. Here we listen to the thunder's roll and mark the lightning's flash as the Law is given at Sinai and a motley crowd of nomads is welded and fused into a nation under the glow of an incandescent faith. We hear "the sound of running history" as we observe the footsteps of God making broad his path in the history of a chosen people. We see the panorama take shape before our eyes. We catch the melodies of singers as they break forth into triumphant praise before the mighty acts of God or rise from the depths in plaintive tones as men bow before the chastening of a righteous God. The seraphic eloquence of Isaiah falls upon our ears and the passionate pleadings of Jeremiah grip our hearts and we catch visions of far-off things yet to be. The stern tirades of the shepherd from Tekoa and the dull moanings of Hosea's broken heart together with the raptured visions of Ezekiel intrigue us strangely and stir our emotions. Nahum in his furious joy at Nineveh destroyed, Zephaniah in his puritanical zeal, Habakkuk on his watchtower, Obadiah with his unrelenting hatred of Edom, Haggai with Zechariah and his visions, and Malachi who seeks to put new life into the restored community—what a variety we have here!

Here, too, are the "wise saws" of ancient sages as they seek to counsel the wayward sons of men and direct them in the path of righteousness and here, too, are those larger utterances of the human spirit in the day of trial when men seek to understand the riddle of the universe and see the face of God. Gospels full of tender benedictions and Epistles replete with spacious argument are here, and Apocalypses that spill the vials of wrath. What a variety the Bible presents! Simple stories from the morning of life when the earth was young and the sons of God sang for very joy in the creating energy of God, records of men in their upward struggle to the fuller light, honest books that reveal man as he really is, man in his defeats and victories, his joys and sorrows, his virtues and vices—what a book is this! The mood of pessimism that finds no meaning in life is present here (Ecclesiastes), and a book that never once mentions the name of God (Esther) and finds its chief joy in telling of a bloody pogrom in reverse, which fortunately has no basis in history. This may not be what we would expect a Bible to be but it has pleased God to give us a Bible just like that.

b) UNITY THROUGH VARIETY

Through all this strange variety there is present a deep underlying unity: one increasing purpose runs through it all. It is this unity of purpose that enables us to speak of the Bible as "the Book." A scarlet thread of divine purpose runs from Genesis to Revelation and binds all these varied volumes into one. The Bible is the record of God's redemptive activity from beginning to end. One or two illustrations will make this clear and we can begin here right at the beginning. There in the opening chapters of Genesis we have the story of the Garden of Eden and at the very end of the book of Revelation we have the story of the garden city of God.

> And he showed me a pure river of water of life, clear as crystal, proceeding out of the throne of God and of the Lamb. In the midst of the street of it, and on either side of the river, was there the tree of life, which bare twelve manner of fruits, and yielded her fruit every month; and the leaves of the tree were for the healing of the nations.
>
> (Revelation 22:1, 2)

So often we read these words, or hear them read, and we fail to comprehend their meaning. For here we have Paradise Regained set over against Paradise Lost, and if we enquire how man is to pass from the latter to the former we open our Bible near the middle and read there of another garden—the Garden of Gethsemane where "we have rest by His sorrow and life by His death." Only as we keep fellowship with him there can we be translated from darkness to light, from Paradise Lost to Paradise Regained. In that sense we might almost say the Bible is a book of gardens:

> The kiss of the sun for pardon,
> The song of the birds for mirth,
> One is nearer God's heart in a garden
> Than anywhere else on earth.   (Dorothy Gurney)

This need not be regarded as fanciful. It can be attested by any attentive reader. Primitive man leads through regular sequence to man redeemed and glorified. Theologians express it in another way and say with the New Testament, "The Lamb was slain from the foundation of the world." That means that Creation was laid on a redemptive basis. The only-begotten Son was in the bosom of the Father from all eternity. Calvary is just the bringing forth into time of something that was in the heart of God before the world was built.

That the New Testament cannot be understood apart from the Old Testament is an elementary axiom in the interpretation of Scripture. We may say here that the Old Testament is the record of a long search while the New Testament is the story of a great find. It is not without reason that the Protestant Reformers placed the Prophets at the close of the Old Testament—Chronicles is the last book in the Hebrew Bible—for they stand like sentinels on watch, waiting for "Him who is to come." That is the typical attitude of the Old Testament saint "waiting for the consolation of Israel." It is the attitude of Daniel with his face pressed against the window looking towards Jerusalem. All these people are on tip-toe with a tense spirit of expectation: they live by faith.

> My soul waiteth for the Lord
> more than they that watch for the morning.
>   (Psalm 130:6)

Behold, as the eyes of servants look unto the
hand of their masters,
and as the eyes of a maiden unto the hand of
her mistress,
So our eyes wait upon the Lord our God.

(Psalm 123:2)

It is this attitude of expectancy that characterises the Old
Testament and finds its fullest expression in the prophets
with their Messianic predictions. It is based on a linear
theory of history that sees events not as mere events but as
the expression of a divine purpose moving to a goal. Such
a view of history is not found outside the Bible and that is
why we are justified in speaking of progressive revelation.
History here does not move, as it moves elsewhere, in circles
or cycles, passing through various ages, golden, silver, iron,
clay, to end in cataclysm and then begin all over again. Not
that the Bible thinks of history as moving in an absolutely
straight line but rather in a spiralling line, sometimes reced-
ing but always moving forward again on a higher level. The
movement is forward and not around: it is linear not cyclical. History to the Hebrew was the sphere in which God's
purpose was unveiled and made known to men. Thus the
Old Testament finds its consummation in the New and the
New finds its explanation in the Old. To use the words of
Augustine:

Novum Testamentum in Vetere latet;
Vetus Testamentum in Novo patet.
(In the Old Testament the New lies concealed,
In the New Testament the Old is revealed.)

Without the New Testament the Old would be but a shape-
less torso ending in the sterilities of the Talmud: without the
Old Testament the New would be an inexplicable riddle.
Each is incomplete without the other. Thus we find the

same sentinel attitude in the case of Anna and Simeon (Luke
2) who stand at the end of the old and the beginning of the
new dispensation. It has "the sound of a grand Amen" when
Simeon says:

> Now lettest thou thy servant depart in peace, according to
> thy word: for mine eyes have seen thy salvation.
>
> (Luke 2:29, 30)

Life has nothing more to offer to the man who has seen the
salvation of the Lord.

We may approach this from another angle and say that
the Old Testament represents religion in the interrogative
mood while the New Testament represents it in its positive
and glorious affirmations. Thus again the connection is made
clear. The Old Testament cries, "How long, O Lord, how
long" or more poignantly "My God, my God, why?". The
New Testament shouts in the joy of a great discovery,
"Thanks be unto God through our Lord Jesus Christ." The
Old Testament saint is

> An infant crying in the night,
> An infant crying for the light,
> And with no language but a cry.   (Tennyson)

The New Testament saint stands in the fulness of light and
all shadows are passed away.

The whole sacrificial system of the Old Testament, it would
not be too much to say, is but a searching and groping after
complete knowledge of, and communion with, God. In the
New Testament the search is ended and men rejoice as those
who "have found great spoil." One of the most thrilling
stories in the Old Testament is the story of Abraham and
Isaac in Genesis 22. We may use it by way of illustration.

> And it came to pass after these things, that God did tempt

(i.e. make trial of) Abraham . . ., And he said unto him, Take now thy son, thine only son, Isaac, whom thou lovest, and get thee into the land of Moriah; and offer him there for a burnt offering . . . And Abraham took the wood of the burnt offering, and laid it upon Isaac his son; and he took the fire in his hand, and a knife; and they went both of them together. And Isaac spake unto his father: and he said, My father: And he said, Here am I, my son. And he said, Behold the fire and the wood: but where is the lamb for a burnt offering? (Genesis 22:1, 2, 6, 7)

The Hebrew shows a strange austerity of speech here, a wonderful economy of words, but every word is weighted full. Whether one reads that story in Hebrew or in English one cannot fail to feel the extreme weight of passion and pathos here. The repeated emphasis, *thy son, thine only son, Isaac, whom thou lovest,* shows by its halting, limping form the dreadful thing that was laid upon the heart of Abraham. Not that the Hebrew lingers over emotion or makes play upon the feelings: Hollywood would have shown us something here! They would have made more of that story but in so doing they would have marred its undying beauty. A whole vast ocean of grief is here and the language trembles with emotion. The innocent prattle of the child must have sounded like the knell of doom to the father's breaking heart. But the Hebrew says nothing of all that. And though this story was first written for another purpose than the later editor had in view it expresses for us the very spirit of the whole Old Testament. "Where is the lamb?" is the cry of that volume and it echoes through the Old Testament and underlies all the zeal of the sacrificial system. It finds its answer when on that day John the Baptist stands with two of his disciples and sees One approaching of whom he can say, "Behold the Lamb" (John 1:29). The age-long quest has ended and man's long search has reached the great discovery. In the New Testament men are leaping and dancing and praised God. All theology is fused into doxology. "Worthy is the Lamb," "Behold what manner of love!" "Thanks be unto God"—these are the key phrases of the New Testament. And that is why the New Testament is the most radiant hymnbook ever written. Men sing when they arrive for their joy is full. The Law was "our schoolmaster to bring us to Christ" and men rejoiced that it had found its consummation. "The testimony of Jesus is the spirit of prophecy" (Revelation 9:10). For the Jew the Old Testament ran to seed in the Talmud: for the Christian it blossomed into the Gospel of the grace of God.

c) FALSE INTERPRETATIONS TO BE AVOIDED

We have laid such stress on this matter of inner unity and organic connection of Old and New Testaments because, frequently and wrongly, the unity is sought in other ways which destroy the real vitality of Scriptures. The connection is not rigid and mechanical but vital and dynamic. Frequently, however, the Old Testament is regarded as the New Testament in hieroglyphics and allegorical interpretations and a theology of types read into the Old Testament ideas and doctrines that are not to be found there and which are foreign to the Hebrew and impossible to his way of thinking. Exegesis, which means *leading out* what is in the text, gives place to Eisegesis which *leads into* the text things that are not there. The time has really come for fair play towards the Bible. It must be allowed to speak for itself. We must cease to impose our ideas upon it and just listen to what it is saying. The prophetic insight of the prophets which enabled them to see to the roots and realities of things and to discern eternal principles in temporary and transient situations has too often been changed into the far sight of the stargazer who spoke of things that had no relevance to the people whom the speaker addressed. Thus the book of Daniel in the Old Testament and the book of Revelation in the New Testament have become the happy hunting-grounds of all the fools and fanatics who fancy they see the number of the Beast on the forehead of Stalin and identify the Kremlin at Moscow with the great image on the plain of Dura. Such extravagances are still common and are to be regretted: they reduce the Bible to a volume of conundrums and turn it into a kind of crossword puzzle.

"The letter killeth, but the spirit giveth life" (II Corinthians 3:6). This cannot be emphasized too much or too often. It is worthwhile lingering over this matter for a moment. An earlier age was accustomed to providing the truth of Christianity by pointing to the miracles in the Gospel stories and the prophecies of the Old Testament. But he would be a bold man who would essay that line of apologetic today: conditions have changed entirely. People are not disposed to accept miracles readily and it is the fashion to regard the prophets as characterized by insight rather than foresight or farsight. Such an antithesis as this may not be pressed too far, for insight need not exclude foresight. In the case of the prophets it did not. No one will deny that there is much genuine prediction in the Old Testament and no one will deny that a great many of these predictions were unfulfilled. If the Prophets were to be judged by their power to predict, most of them would shrink very considerably in stature. These Prophets were primarily men who spoke for God and they spoke to the people of their own time in reference to the needs and demands of their contemporary situation. "Religion," says A. S. Peake, "is not, as used to be thought, a matter to be received on credentials, for, as Hort said, what do they prove but themselves? We have now taken the weight of our apologetic from the external and thrown it upon the intrinsic value. Unless the Gospel is true for its own sake argument from prophecy or miracle will do little nowadays to establish its credit. The temper of our times is too impatient of our proofs."[1]

It is this "temper of our times" we have to meet. The divinity of Christ may not be proved by the miracles or the prophecies. But it may be that the *miracles can be proved by the Person of Christ* and Christ may be seen to be the fulfillment of prophecy.

Nor will we enhance the Person of our Lord by adducing a series of proof-texts as does the writer of Matthew's Gospel. Matthew is the most Jewish of all the Gospel writers and he reveals a leading characteristic of Judaism in his stress upon the letter. "That all righteousness might be fulfilled" or "that it might be fulfilled which was spoken by the prophets"—these formulae recur with such frequency that one might almost think Jesus lived his life according to some external program. Nothing, however, could be further from the truth: Jesus was moved from within, wholly free, spontaneous, and inspired in all his words and actions. There was nothing in his life of the mechanical or formal so that his movements and actions could be calculated in advance. The very use of such texts in Matthew shows the danger of this method. "Out of Egypt have I called my son" (Matthew 2:15) is from Hosea and refers, without question, to Israel: the reference, too, is inappropriate, for in the original oracle the prophet proceeds to chide and rebuke the people for their apostasy. In Matthew 2:23 we have a reference to an Old

[1] A. S. Peake, *The Bible, Its Origin, Significance and Abiding Worth* (1913), p. 362.

Testament oracle which is not to be found at all in the volume while in 27:9 we have an oracle attributed to Jeremiah though it actually occurs in Zechariah (Zechariah 11:12). Too great stress may not be laid upon the letter: the glowing spirit is that which vitalizes Scripture.

While we are contending here that Jesus was far too vital, original, and inspired to live according to a prepared program or to have his life directed by external authority, it is worthy of note that on particular occasions he did set himself deliberately in line with Old Testament prophecy and fulfill it before the eyes of the people. Such an occasion was the triumphal entry into Jerusalem on Palm Sunday (Matthew 21:7). Here he linked himself with the popular expectation and set himself forth as the fulfillment of Old Testament prediction. But *he does this of his own initiative and not by external constraint.* Normally, however, it is otherwise. If he assumes the role of the Suffering Servant (Isaiah 53) and if men assign that role to him, no one will argue that literal fulfillment is involved here, for all that is said of the Suffering Servant cannot be interpreted in detail of Jesus. The church, indeed, was guided by a sound instinct when it referred the prophecy contained in Isaiah 53 to the sufferings of Christ but *the identity is not of the letter but of the spirit.* "The great argument from prophecy," says Peake,

> is that which views the whole history of Israel as moving steadily forward to its climax in the Gospel.[2]

This is the *linear* theory of history. The prophets were dynamic men with nothing mechanical about them. And Jesus is greater than the prophets. To treat the Old Testament as a collection of proof-texts is to miss the vital spirit and fail in our interpretation of the living facts of history.

[2] A. S. Peake, *op. cit.,* p. 368.

d) FORMATION OF THE CANON

How these various and varied books were brought together to form our Bible and constitute "the Book" is an
interesting story. We speak in this connection of the *Canon*
of the Old Testament and the *Canon* of the New Testament.
The word "canon" comes to us through the Greek which
took it from the Hebrew and the word means a measuring
line or standard. The books had to measure up to a certain
standard before they were deemed worthy of being admitted
to the sacred collection and dignified with the title "canonical." And here precisely is the place where we see *the human element in the origin of the Bible*. The judgment as to
which writings should be considered canonical was made
by mortal men. Moreover, various groups of men at various
times have held different views as to which writings should
be set in the Canon. The Church of Rome has a larger Canon
than the Protestant Church. The Canon of the Old Testament as we know it in the Authorized Version and most
modern translations is the Hebrew Canon as finally adopted
at Jamnia about 90 A.D. The Greek Canon, which is that of
the Roman Church, is larger and includes those books which
we call the *Apocrypha*. This word is the Greek term for
"hidden" or "concealed." Thus we note that from the beginning there has been quite a variety of opinions as to the
number and nature of the sacred books. The Protestant Reformers took a decisive line in this matter and they took
that line in opposition to the Roman Church. They adopted
the Hebrew Canon as it was fixed by the council of Jewish
rabbis at Jamnia and that is the form in which we normally have our Bible. Some Protestant Bibles include the
Apocrypha: the Church of England includes those "hidden

books" but it does not derive doctrine from them. Now the principle adopted by the Protestant Reformers, that only books written in Hebrew (and Aramaic) should be admitted to the Canon, was not a sound principle. But it was adopted and our Authorized Version represents the Hebrew Canon although the order of the books in the English version is not that of the Hebrew. Apart from this matter of the order of the books our Old Testament corresponds to that of the Hebrew, ancient or modern. Whether the Synod of Jamnia included too much or too little is matter for debate, but the fact remains that the books we have in our Old Testament were selected and canonized by human authority. To say that is not to deny that they may have been guided by the spirit of God in the choice they made. There is reason to believe that they were so guided.

e) THE PROCESS OF CANONIZATION

It is important here to distinguish between formal canonization and the steps that precede and lead to the formal act. "To canonize the Scriptures," says T. W. Manson,

> is to recognise something that is there before the Church says so.[3]

The Synod of Jamnia, about 90 A.D., is the only definite date we have in this question of the Old Testament Canon and even here the exact year is uncertain. The date is more or less approximate. There are numerous legends and traditions from earlier periods but they have little or no value for the historian. Before 90 A.D. no one could be certain as to which books were canonical, and even after the Synod of Jamnia the judgment of the Rabbis was frequently called in question. For there will always be those who are unwilling to

[3] T. W. Manson, *A Companion to the Bible* (1939), p. 11.

accept a judgment that goes against their prejudices or fails to coincide with their thinking. "A man convinced against his will is of the same opinion still." Whatever we may think of the final judgment we can at least trace the steps by which they came to it and we can discern how the Old Testament attained its present form.

From early days a certain sanctity attached to the words of the Law as given by the priest in the name of God. The people treasured these words; they were engraven on the public memory. They may even have been written down at an early stage of Hebrew history. Such words as "the ten words" (so the Hebrew speaks of the ten commandments, the Decalogue) won universal regard and there was a general consensus of opinion as to their sanctity. This general consensus of opinion does not constitute canonization though it is the main factor leading to ultimate canonization. That which held of the Law was true also of the Prophets and the songs of the singers and the sayings of the Sages, each perhaps in diminishing degree with reference to sanctity. There was nothing sacrosanct as to the exact form and order of the words—at least in the early period. There are various forms of "the ten words": Exodus 20 and Deuteronomy 5 both give the commandments, but there are remarkable deviations in the two versions so far as the letter is concerned. Men were then content to express the general sense in varying words. Deuteronomy in 621 B.C.—another definite date in history—seems to mark a decisive step forward in the process that led to formal canonization: here we have a book solemnly accepted as regulative of the national life and adopted as the statute of the realm. With this act Israel became a "people of the Book," though that phrase does not necessarily imply that they became a people of God. For, as A. B. Davidson has said:

Deuteronomy and Pharisaism came into the world on the same day.[4]

The process of canonization was not without its dangerous elements. We may pass by this point for the moment and only call attention to the fact that curses are invoked upon anyone who adds to, or takes from, the content of this book (Deuteronomy 12:32). Such formulae are common enough in ancient legal documents. But these curses did not prevent other codes from emerging and in spite of the curse men were not deterred from adding to and subtracting from their contents. But as we advance towards the later period we find an increasing regard for the letter; the idea of an inviolable text begins to appear. This is certainly characteristic of Judaism after the Exile and the Law becomes more a thing of the letter and less and less consideration is paid to the spirit.

Unfortunately, the historical development here is not clear but one or two things seem reasonably certain. Formerly it was the custom to speak of Ezra as the founder of the Old Testament Canon, but such a view does not seem tenable. History shows that by the time of Ezra—whose date may be 397 B.C., though Albright[5] prefers the date 428 B.C.—the first five books of the Old Testament, commonly called the Pentateuch, had assumed their present form and that the text, as we now have it, had reached a fixed and final form. The Samaritan schism, which took place shortly after Ezra's time, shows the Pentateuch in practically the same form as in the Massoretic or standard Hebrew text. There are minor variations here and there, and there are like variations in the Greek version (LXX) made about the middle of the third

4James Hastings, edited by, *A Dictionary of the Bible,* Vol. II (1900), p. 577.
5W. F. Albright, in *The Jews, Their History, Culture, and Religion,* edited by L. Finkelstein, Vol. I, p. 53.

century B.C. Substantially, these versions represent the same text as we have in our Bible. But there does not appear to have been any formal act of canonization of the Law at this time—though it is frequently maintained that such did take place at this time—but there was that general consensus of opinion as regards its sanctity which must ultimately find expression in the formal act of canonization.

The Law, the Prophets, and the Writings (Hebrew, *Kethubhim;* Greek, *Hagiographa*) represents the usually accepted division of the Old Testament Canon. We have indicated the process in regard to the Law, and the same process is visible in the case of the Prophets and the Writings. The Prophets here include more than we usually associate with that term, for in it are included the early historical books Joshua-Kings, probably on the ground that they were regarded as written by prophets, and those books which we commonly call prophets: Isaiah, Jeremiah, Ezekiel and the book of the Twelve (or Minor) Prophets. A division was made between "the former" and the "the latter" prophets: the historical books constituted the former, while the others, whom we designate the prophets, formed the latter. This division into former and latter may be due to their order in time or their order in the Hebrew Bible. More probably the latter reason is correct. An equal reverence with the Law was not accorded the Prophets as may be gathered from the fact that only one verse of the Law was read at a time by the Targeman (the interpreter who translated the Hebrew into the popular speech) while three verses of a prophet were taken at a time. Nevertheless, from the beginning those words or oracles were regarded as worthy of esteem and the basis was laid for later canonization. By the year 300 B.C. or slightly later the prophetic literature seems to have reached something very like its present form although the text was not fixed and final as in the case of the Law. Additions could be made—and were made—by later editors, but, substantially, they were in the form in which we have them by the close of the third century B.C.

It is in regard to the third division of the Canon, the Writings, that dispute continued right down into the Christian era. These Writings include all that does not fall within the other two groups. The order of the collection varies in the Hebrew and Greek Bibles: in the Hebrew the order is Psalms, Proverbs, Job, Song of Songs, Ruth, Lamentations, Ecclesiastes, Esther, Daniel, Ezra, Nehemiah, I and II Chronicles. It can easily be understood how division of opinion might arise in reference to such a varied collection. The test applied by the Jew to any book with regard to its value was, "Does it defile the hands?" By that he meant, could it be handled like any secular book which might be taken up without any ritual precautions. Or did such a degree of sanctity adhere to the volume that one must put himself in a state of ritual cleanness before handling the holy thing? The question was fiercely agitated in regard to particular works in this collection, specially Ecclesiastes, Esther, and the Song of Songs. Do these "defile the hands"? The division of opinion continued long beyond the date of Jamnia and may even exist in some circles still today. The Song of Songs is probably the most erotic thing in the Bible and it was only by reason of the failure to discern its real nature that it attained to the Canon. Many had serious doubts about its spiritual value but by a subtle allegorizing on the part of the Rabbis, in which they were followed later by the Christian church, the Song of Songs was deemed worthy of a place in the Canon. Ecclesiastes, which is a thoroughgoing piece of scepticism, caused quite a furor. Its popularity, however, could not be questioned, and by a few deft additions and pious interpolations it was dressed in a seeming garb of orthodoxy and made to look more respectable than its author ever meant it to be. It finally "got by" but only by the skin of its teeth. It surely would have been matter for regret for if it had not made the grade, for a Bible that is intended to be the book of Everyman should not fail to represent the mood of scepticism. We can recognize here a Providential guidance of those who gave us the Canon. At the same time we may regret that such a noble volume as the book of Ecclesiasticus was not admitted, for the gentle son of Sira is more worthy than Qoheleth. It is one of the ironies of history that he was known only in the Greek form until the beginning of this century when about two-thirds of the original Hebrew text was discovered in a *geniza* (Jewish burial chamber). Esther, too, had a rough passage to the final resting-place in the Canon: this is the more surprising as Esther is the most Jewish book in the Old Testament. But it failed to mention the name of God—in that sense we may call it a Godless book —and that did not commend it to the Rabbis at Jamnia. But its intense nationalism, and its association with the joyous, boisterous feast of Purim secured its final admission. In these trying times for the Jew we need not grudge them the book of Esther though the Christian may find little spiritual sustenance in it. Best known, perhaps, are the words of Mordecai:

> Who knoweth whether thou art come to the kingdom for such a time as this?   (Esther 4:14)

This group of Writings seems to have been in a fairly fluid state until near the close of the second Christian century and long after the date of Jamnia disputes continued to center around these books, especially the three just referred to, and many refused to accept the committee's decision. But at Jamnia the Canon had been finally fixed and the form and contents of the Old Testament were determined.

f) CANON OF THE NEW TESTAMENT

We will bring this chapter to a close with a brief consideration of the Canon of the New Testament. Luke in his opening verse tells us many had undertaken to write Gospels but it is not difficult to understand why we have only four in our New Testament. There were, too, many more Epistles than are preserved to us in the New Testament, but we have only those that were deemed worthy of a place in the Canon. A glance at a book like M. R. James' *The Apocryphal New Testament*[6] will reveal that we have in our New Testament only a selection from early Christian literature. In this book by Dr. James we will find Gospels by Thomas, Peter, Philip, a Gospel of the Ebionites and a Gospel of the Egyptians. Here, too, are the Acts of John, the Acts of Paul, the Acts of Peter, together with the Acts of Andrew and the Acts of Thomas. Also here are the letters of Christ and Abgarus, the letter of Lentulus, and also the Epistle of the Apostles. We have also Apocalypses from Thomas, Peter, and Paul. Quite a variety! But we have only to look at them to see why they did not find admission to our New Testament and to see the difference between canonical and uncanonical. Take this from the Gospel of Thomas:

> And after some days as Jesus walked with Joseph through the city, there ran one of the children and smote Jesus on the arms: but Jesus said unto him: So finish thou thy course. And immediately he fell to the earth and died.[7]

[6]Oxford, 1924.
[7]M. R. James, *op. cit.,* p. 60.

Or look at this story which is perhaps a little less repulsive:

> And Jesus came to be eight years old. Now Joseph was a builder, and wrought ploughs and yokes for oxen. And one day a certain rich man said unto Joseph; Sir, make me a bed serviceable and comely. But Joseph was troubled because the beam which he had made ready for the work was short. Jesus said unto him: Be not troubled, but take thou hold of this beam by the one and and I by the other, and let us draw it out. And so it came to pass, and forthwith Joseph found it serviceable for that which he had desired.[8]

It is easy to see the difference between the canonical Gospels and these uncanonical or Apocryphal Gospels. We can *feel* the difference.

During the First World War the Bank of England was forced to employ a great many women in place of men who had gone into service with the armed forces. One such young woman was assigned the task of detecting counterfeit notes. The Bank of England note is exceedingly difficult to counterfeit. This young lady had to go through piles of those large bills and the thing was getting on her nerves: she was near a nervous collapse. One day the superior officer of the bank saw her on the verge of tears and sought to comfort her. "Don't worry," he said, "when you come to a 'phoney' you will know it by the touch." It is this crinkliness of the paper that is so difficult to counterfeit: the touch instinctively discerns the difference when a counterfeit appears. So it is with the Gospels. People knew them "by the touch." The religious and aesthetic sense rebelled against such stories as represented Jesus as a petulant little brat or a mere wonderworker. They said "this is not the Jesus we know." Certain things were consonant with his Person, but not these things.

[8]*Ibid.*, p. 63.

And so these Gospels were set aside as unworthy of the Person of Christ.

So with the letters of Paul. People knew Paul and what he stood for. Each church carefully preserved his epistles and they were quoted as authoritative. Church would trade copies with church until the whole corpus of correspondence was in being. There were other writings of which men thought highly and in the Codex Sinaiticus the *Epistle of Barnabas* appears as part of the New Testament, as does also a favorite writing entitled *The Shepherd of Hermas*.

It is not our purpose here to discuss this in full detail but rather in its main outlines and it may suffice here to say that in the year 367 A.D. Athanasius in his Paschal Letter set forth the Canon of the New Testament exactly as we have it and this was accepted in the East. At the Council of Carthage in 397 A.D. the West came to the same decision and by the close of the fourth century A.D. the New Testament was fixed in the form which we now have, though for another century doubts were freely and frequently expressed as to the admission to the Canon of the General (or Catholic) Epistles and the Apocalypse. These hesitations were most common in Asia Minor and among the Syriac-speaking churches. The Quini-Sextine Council, held at Constantinople in 692 A.D., confirmed the Canon for East and West but, strangely enough, no Ecumenical Council has ever rendered a decision on the matter.

As to the principles employed in deciding upon a Canon of the New Testament these were similar to those used to determine the Canon of the Old Testament. It was held that to be qualified for admission a writing must be by an apostle: in practice this was widened to include associates of apostles and without this widening we would not have had the Gospels of Mark or Luke. Again it was required that each writing should conform in its teaching to the generally accepted rule of faith as that was understood by the church at large. Finally each writing had to be vouched for by one or more of the leading churches. As in the case of the Old Testament there was peculiar difficulty about some writings that seemed worthy but did not fully conform to canonical requirements. The Epistle to the Hebrews presented such problems but these were solved by a kind of "gentleman's agreement" and by a polite fiction that writing was set among the Epistles of Paul. Thus the New Testament finally attained its present form and our Bible was completed.

III

Wise Men and Fools

THE WISDOM LITERATURE of the Old Testament includes the books of Proverbs, Job, and Ecclesiastes. Several Psalms (1, 37, 49, 73, 78, 91, 126) also fall within this category. Outside the Canon of the Old Testament the best-known work is that of Jesus ben Sirach, commonly called Ecclesiasticus (circa 190 B.C.). It is much to be regretted, as we have seen above, that this book was excluded from the Canon for it has elements of great value. It failed to find admission to the Canon because it was known only in the Greek version but within recent years it has been recovered, in large part, in its original Hebrew form. The Greek translation was made by the author's nephew about 132 B.C. Occasional reference will be made to this book in the course of our discussion in order that we may have a clear idea of the growth and development of Hebrew Wisdom Literature.

Wisdom Literature is not peculiar to Israel. It is a universal phenomenon in ancient as in modern life. Gnomic poetry has its roots in life and everywhere we find such gnomes and proverbs. These are often assembled and used as a means of popular instruction. Such proverbs hold a mirror up to life and reveal the quality of a people. Tribal and national morality can be evaluated by a study of proverbs in any particular group, and the development of a people may be measured by a study of its Wisdom writings. These proverbs speak the language of common life and reflect the soul of the group or nation. "Waste not, want not" is a Scottish proverb and expresses with crystal clarity a side of that national character that, by general admission, needs no emphasis. "Revenge is a morsel for God" or "Revenge of a hundred years old hath still its sucking teeth" plainly attest their origin in the hot-blooded Italian. "Thy speech bewrayeth thee" may be said of proverbs as it was said of Peter's Galilean accent. A study of proverbs, ancient and modern, would afford food for thought—and more proverbs.

The earliest forms of this literature are found in Egypt and reach as far back as the third millennium B.C. By a fortunate chance these writings have been preserved to us; they were used as manuals of instruction in the schools of later centuries. They formed the headlines in copybooks for those seeking to learn reading and writing. That schoolboys were as careless then as now is evident from the many errors appearing in their papers. The wise sayings of Ptah-hotep, a high official of the fifth dynasty (circa 2450 B.C.), were copied and recopied and the results are with us to this day.[1] Ptah-hotep himself had made good in the civil service and he is concerned to train suitable successors. What he writes he refers to as ancient wisdom already known long before his time. From him we have a philosophy of success by one who has succeeded and wishes to point the way for others. Expressed in pithy sentences these maxims of his counsel to culture, self-restraint, obedience, and fidelity. Here we have "the harvest of the quiet eye" and if it seems to us only prudential morality the same may be said of the book of

[1] John A. Wilson, *Ancient Near Eastern Texts,* edited by J. B. Pritchard, (1950), pp. 412 ff.

Proverbs. "Wine, women, and song" lead to ruin: there is no royal road to success.

> If thou art a poor fellow, following a man of distinction, one of good standing with the god, know thou not his former insignificance. Thou shouldst not be puffed-up against him because of what thou didst know of him formerly. Show regard for him in conformance with what has accrued to him—property does not come of itself. It is their law for him who wishes them. *As for him who oversteps, he is feared.* It is god who makes (a man's) quality, and he defends him (even) while he is asleep.[2]

This might look a little like Lord Chesterfield giving a philosophy of success, teaching how to win friends and influence people. But there is no cynicism in this sage's tone, only a profound awareness of the necessity of sound principles in the handling of life and the great business of living.

The land of Egypt offered a congenial environment for the growth of this type of literature. It was otherwise, however, in Babylon. Here the circumstances did not favor such development. The Babylonians were engaged in big business and large-scale commerce. Multifarious action left little time for reflection. The sage did not flourish here. Religion tended to become mechanized into a thing of ritual and magic where soothsayers and ritual priests found ample employment. But one fragment from the library of an Assyrian king can be quoted: it owes its survival to the same happy chance that gave us the sayings of Ptah-hotep. This also the schoolboys copied in their copy-books.

> Slander not, speak fair:
> Say no evil, speak good:
> He who slanders and speaks evil,
> From him shall the god Shamash exact requital.

[2]J. A. Wilson, *ibid.,* p. 413.

> Open not thy mouth wide, guard thy lips,
> When thou art wroth speak not forthwith:
> When thou swearest in haste thou mayst repent at leisure,
> And in silence thou wilt feel remorse.[3]

If the god Shamash were not named here one might well assume this was from the book of Proverbs.

That Israel may have been indebted to alien sources for some of her Wisdom Literature is not to be denied. One collection within the book of Proverbs (22:17–24:22) seems to be heavily and directly indebted to the Wisdom of Amenem-ope (dated in the eighth-seventh century B.C.) and Psalm 104 shows that indebtedness to alien sources was no unusual thing. But it seems desirable, in the first instance, to consider the origins of this literature in the national genius. The making of proverbs is a spontaneous activity native to every civilization. Israel is no exception in this matter.

The Wisdom Literature of the Old Testament is largely associated with Solomon, as the Law is associated with Moses and Psalmody with David. Solomon, we read,

> spake three thousand proverbs . . . and he spake of trees, from the cedar tree that is in Lebanon even unto the hyssop that springeth out of the wall: he spake also of beasts, and of fowl, and of creeping things, and of fishes.
>
> (I Kings 4:32, 33)

Solomon appears to have been catholic in his interests and comprehensive in his sympathies. He was a magnificent patron of the arts, and as he brought a wife from Egypt he was probably partial to Egyptian wisdom. Sellin holds that here was a main channel for the inflow of Egyptian influence.[4] Solomon may have brought teachers of wisdom from

---

[3]Hugo Gressmann, *Altorientalische Texte zum Alten Testament* (1926), p. 293.

[4]E. Sellin, *Einleitung in das Alte Testament,* 8th Auflage (1950), p. 156.

Egypt. But wisdom in Israel is older than Solomon. We can pass back of this date to earlier manifestations in the life of the Hebrew people. Wisdom had its home in the east and "the children of the east" are the wise *par excellence*

> Is wisdom no more in Teman?
> Is counsel perished from the prudent?
> Is their wisdom vanished?   (Jeremiah 49:7)

The wisdom of the "children of the east" is known to the writer of I Kings 4:30 while the great book of Job has its setting in the same quarter.

b) PROVERBS AND RIDDLES

The desert heritage of Israel is a most important factor here and whatever other influences may have affected Israel we must not neglect this background. In the desert there was ample leisure for reflection and the long fasts to which the desert dweller was inured lent to the mind a swift detachment from the things of sense. Faculties were strangely sharpened here and a strong self-regarding instinct developed without which the nomad could not survive. Experiences were interrogated and integrated into experience and wisdom was acquired in most concrete and living fashion. There was constant conflict between men and wild beasts and wilder men. Thus wisdom found expression in realistic form and proverbs were born. These popular proverbs, like their literary successors, were intended to inculcate practical wisdom; they embody the distilled thought and reflection of countless generations. "Two dogs killed a lion" is the nomad's practical and living expression of our abstract word: "Union is strength." The empirical basis of the simple Arabic word is clear as it is concrete. That is the wisdom of the east, the wisdom that flourishes in more polished form in Solomon's palace: it never allows us to forget its original habitat nor does it lose its homespun features.

The Hebrew word for proverb is *mashal,* and the meaning of the root is "to lay one thing alongside another," to compare. As a literary term it is applied in the Old Testament to other forms of composition and the original meaning receded into the background. The book of Proverbs in Hebrew is called *Mishelé Shelomo,* the proverbs of Solomon, though many of the sayings in that book show little or nothing of the element of comparison. "Like Nimrod, a mighty hunter before the Lord" is a very simple and ancient form of *mashal.* The three thousand that Solomon is reputed to have spoken were doubtless much more polished and perfect, but whether any of these have survived is doubtful: the book of Proverbs shows what they may have been like.

> As cold waters to a thirsty soul,
> so is good news from a far country,
>
> (Proverbs 25:25)

> As clouds and wind without rain,
> so is he that boasts of gifts ungiven.
>
> (Proverbs 25:14)

The first early attempt at a wisecrack on the part of a village wit and the perfected literary productions of a Solomon are dignified with the name *mashal.* In the later literary productions much of the earlier wisdom is incorporated.

Inasmuch as our prime concern is with the vitality of Scripture it will not be out of place here to consider what a proverb really is. The Oxford dictionary defines it as: "a short pithy saying in general use, adage, saw."

That will do to begin with. Perhaps we might add the

definition given by Lord Russell who says a proverb is "the wit of one and the wisdom of many." Here both origin and function are indicated. Best of all, we shall turn to the finest book ever written about proverbs, *Proverbs and Their Lessons* by Archbishop R. C. Trench, published in the year 1857. This is a notable volume and difficult to acquire in these days for it is long out of print. But it is a veritable gold mine and in what we are about to say we will be largely indebted to it. Certain qualities, he says, must adhere to the saying before it graduates to the class of proverbs and attains the ranks of the elect. Firstly, it must be brief, for "brevity is the soul of wit." Thus the Oxford dictionary is correct in saying, "a short saying." Secondly, it must have *sense:* that means it must not be so compressed that its meaning cannot be grasped immediately. "Forewarned, forearmed" is short as can be and it has sense. "Extremes meet" also satisfies requirements. Classical proverbs often suffer from undue compression but *"amantes amentes"* (lovers are mad) is clear enough. The Greek *"mēden agan"* was as clear to the Greek as is to us: "moderation in all things." Thirdly, the proverb must have *salt,* that is, a distinct tang or flavor, the element of pungency that gives it "kick." These three elements must be present in a proverb, and there is yet a fourth element without which a proverb cannot be. That is the element of popularity. The cute remark, for all its sense and salt, will fall stillborn to the ground if it is not caught up and repeated by the bystanders. It must be endorsed by public acceptance and repeated through the generations before it becomes a real *mashal.* Many a word that seemed worthy has wasted its sweetness on the desert air because it failed to find public acceptance and become popular. Thus we may say that proverbs are born and not made; the proverb has no author. "Is

Saul also among the prophets?" Who first said that? We cannot tell, though we would like to know. It does not matter, but that day a proverb was born and the wit of one became the wisdom of many. We are unconscious of any debt here. Proverbs are common property and belong to the world. There is no copyright in them. Proverbs, moreover, are the plain man's argument for with a proverb on his lips a man may well feel he stands upon a rock and the wisdom of the ancients is with him. The concentrated experience of the generations is at his side.

Proverbs strike home to the heart and clinch a matter beyond a peradventure. "What has the chaff to do with the wheat?" (Jeremiah 23:28)—yea, what? A man might well consider the case closed beyond any possibility of reopening when he had cited such a *mashal*. "As saith the proverb of the ancients, Wickedness proceedeth from the wicked" (I Samuel 24:13). No one can gainsay that. Such usage, of course, might suggest the tyranny of the dead hand and may look suspiciously like what Dr. Johnson referred to as "knocking down your adversary with the butt end of the pistol." Nevertheless these proverbs live and are full of vitality; they spring from life and speak to life. The present writer has good reason to remember a word spoken by a wise father: "Let not him who girdeth on *his armor* boast himself as he that putteth it off" (I Kings 20:11). If we heard that on the radio we would sit up and take notice and assume it was "The Voice of Experience" speaking. And so it is: many generations have ratified that word. It took its seat among the immortals thousands of years ago. Such words are as "apples of gold in baskets of silver"—to use the faulty translation of the Authorized Version—and we know not who first gave utterance to them. Perhaps some bearded warrior sitting in his house of hair in the desert or some wise woman of Tekoa to whom the commander-in-chief had recourse when he was at his wits' end (II Samuel 14:1–14).

A second and more developed form of the earlier Wisdom Literature may be seen in the popular riddle (*chida*), of which Samson's riddle (Judges 14:12–18) is the best known example. The putting forth of riddles seems to have been a form of social entertainment and it must have contributed something of an intellectual element to gatherings that otherwise might be dull enough. Weddings may be of interest to the main parties concerned, but they may be boring and tedious to the spectators. On the occasion of Samson's wedding we have the actual riddle given and it is enlivened with "apt alliteration's artful aid":

Me hă'okel yatsà ma'ăkal	Out of the feeder come forth food
Ume 'az yatsa' matok	And sweetness from the strong.

The answer is given in the form of a question—and this question may really be another riddle requiring the answer "Love"—and it runs thus:

Ma matok middĕbash	What's sweeter than honey?
Ume 'az me 'ări	And what's stronger than a lion?

The boisterous fun of this particular occasion is rendered more exuberant by Samson's rude response, which itself again may be an ancient proverb:

Lulu chărashtem bĕ'eglathi	If with my heifer ye did not plow
Lo mĕtsathem chidathi	You had not solved my riddle now.

Our knowledge of social life in ancient Israel is somewhat scanty but such incidents let in a flood of light.

That such customs were not confined to common folk is clear from the story of the Queen of Sheba (I Kings 10:1 ff.)

who came to "prove Solomon with hard questions" (*chidoth,* riddles). The practice of wisdom and the putting forth of riddles or "dark sayings" (Psalm 49:4) appear to have gone hand in hand. The *mashal* and the *chida* constituted the stock-in-trade of the ancient sage. In I Kings 3:16–28 we have a most interesting example of wisdom at work and King Solomon is called upon to solve a real knotty problem. Two mothers contend for the possession of the living child—whose child is it? "Bring me a sword," says the king, "and let the child be divided," whereupon the anguished cry of the real mother enables the king to come to the obvious decision. This story was a popular favorite and it is found in twenty-two ancient versions throughout the ancient world! There is reason to think it originated in India: such stories are notorious travelers. An interesting parallel from modern life is given by Kent:

> The life of the Arabian desert presents many striking parallels. Two women were brought before a famous judge among the Arabs, charged with shamelessness. After listening to the charge, the judge pronounced the following sentence: *Let her who is innocent of this charge throw aside her garment and stand before me naked.* One woman unhesitatingly carried out the terms of the sentence. The other cast herself to the ground before the judge, crying. *Slay me instead.* It requires no imagination to determine which woman was declared innocent.[5]

c) WISDOM AND THE SCHOOLS

Wisdom to the Hebrew, as might be inferred from the foregoing, was a very practical thing. It was a means to an end. Wisdom meant capacity: to be wise is to possess the

[5]C. F. Kent, *The Growth and Contents of the Old Testament* (1926), p. 258.

requisite capacity for a particular task. Thus it is the quality of the soldier (Proverbs 21:22) and it is possessed by technical workers, such as dressmakers (Exodus 28:3), spinning-women (Exodus 35:6), brass-workers (I Kings 7:14), skilled craftsmen (Isaiah 40:20), while it is also the mark and token of a prime minister (Genesis 41:33, 39) and of a popular leader like Joshua (Deuteronomy 34:9). It is that quality which enables a people to live as a nation whose God is the Lord (Deuteronomy 4:6) and without wisdom a king cannot be what he should be (Isaiah 11:2). For lack of wisdom the times are doomed to instability (Isaiah 33:6).

The speculative element which we normally associate with wisdom is conspicuous by its absence. That element does not appear in the Old Testament writings until the Hebrew genius was crossed with the Greek to become "sicklied o'er with the pale cast of thought" and issue in such a mongrel work as Ecclesiastes. This element did not prevail in Hebrew Wisdom Literature: the end in which the Hebrews were interested was life and the main business of living. "To the sages," says Bewer,

> Wisdom meant that sagacity and commonsense which enables man to live a happy and prosperous life.[6]

Now the law of supply and demand operated here as elsewhere. Wisdom was in demand and schools arose to meet the demand. Such schools, as already indicated, existed in Egypt at a very early time. While we have no knowledge of their presence in Israel at an early date—the Old Testament writings were finally assembled by a priestly group who had no great interest in the sages—it may be inferred from certain casual references that such institutions did exist in Israel (II Samuel

[6] J. A. Bewer, *Literature of the Old Testament* (1944), p. 310.

1:18). These schools may have been mainly for "career men" as in Egypt and their teaching may have been of a definitely secular type inculcating worldly wisdom and prudential morality. The products of such schools may have been men like Ahithophel (II Samuel 16:15, 23), Shebna (II Kings 18:37), and Pashur (Jeremiah 20:1), slippery men who mingled in the greasy arena of party politics and kept their eye on the main chance. The generally unfavorable view of the prophets in regard to these samples is easily understood:

> Woe to them that are wise in their own eyes,
> and prudent in their own sight.   (Isaiah 5:21; 29:14)

One of the earliest sections of the Book of Proverbs (25–27) seems to reflect this type of teaching and it resembles that of Ptah-hotep. Proverbs 22:17–24:22 is usually regarded as borrowed from the *Wisdom of Amen-em-ope* (circa 700 B.C.). Etiquette, general deportment, and prudential morality are all commingled here:

> Anything from the details of a farm to the duties of a king towards his subjects commanded the sages' consideration, provided the interests of humanity were involved.[7]

Nothing human was alien to their interest; the world was their parish and they were concerned with life and the way of living.

> Claim not honor in the presence of the king,
> and stand not in the place of great men:
> Better that it should be said unto thee, "Come up hither"
> than that thou shouldst be humbled before the prince.
> (Proverbs 25:6, 7)

That word may have been in the mind of our Lord when he counseled men against occupying the chief seats at a ban-

---

[7] C. F. Kent, *Wise Men of Israel and Their Proverbs*, p. 26.

quet (Luke 14:10). The Scots have a proverb, *"Flee laich, flee lang"* (fly low, fly long) and it catches the spirit of the ancient sage. Evidently the high-flying socialite is an ubiquitous phenomenon. "Enough is as good as a feast" is English but it is not half as expressive as the Hebrew:

> Hast thou found honey? Eat so much as is sufficient for thee, lest thou be filled therewith and vomit it.   (Proverbs 25:16)

Or again—can this be one of the three thousand spoken by Solomon?—let us hear this:

> Better to dwell in the corner of the house top,
> than with a brawling woman, and in a wide house.
> (Proverbs 25:24)

One touch of sympathy makes the whole world kin! We could spare many of these proverbs but not that one. Here we feel our continuity with the generations; such a word speaks home to the heart of Everyman.

A prominent Scot once suggested that the human race could be divided into three classes, "jolly good fellows," "silly asses," and "swine." There is no record of such classification in Scripture, but it is the business of schools to classify their pupils. The sages had a simple classification: men were wise or they were fools. There are, however, fools and fools: some fools are swinish and some are just plain asinine. The task of the schools then, as now, was not so much to work out of human nature "the ape and tiger" as to expel the donkey. The varying words for *fool* in Hebrew might suggest an unfavorable verdict on ancient Hebrew society, but it may have been as Jane Addams said about America, that there are not more fools here than elsewhere but the fools here are all organized! It will reward us here to look first at those pupils of the sages, the raw material on which they had to work and on whom they had to expend their pedagogical gifts. This we shall do by a brief examination of the various terms used for *fool* in the book of Proverbs.

d) THE FOOL IN PROVERBS

It is important to distinguish terms here. While folly is a defect, there are varying forms of that defect. The wise teacher will study his pupils and their defects.

The least harmful and most frequent type of fool is the simpleton (*Pethi*). The term *Pethi* means "Open" and thus signifies one who is open and accessible. He is easily approached and open to any influence. It all depends on who gets him first: he is open to the solicitations of Madame Folly but open also to the appeal of the sage. He is full of possibilities; he can be taken in hand and molded to good or evil, wisdom or folly. He is pliable, he may become a "jolly good fellow," or he may associate with "swine." Thus the teacher announces his aim:

> To give prudence to the simpletons (*Pĕthaim*)
> To the youth knowledge and discretion.   (Proverbs 1:4)

He is young, without experience, but teachable. There is hope for him, and the sage will not miss the opportunity. But boys do not go willingly to school; the simpleton may not want instruction:

> How long, ye simpletons, will ye love simplicity?
> (Proverbs 1:22)

Naturally the will of such a simpleton is weak and he is easily seduced from the path of rectitude. He is open to attack and may surrender basely:

I beheld among the simpletons (*Pĕthaim*),
I discerned among the youths,
a young man void of understanding (*Chaser leb*)
Passing through the street near her house,
and he went his way to her (the harlot's) house.

(Proverbs 7:7, 8)

Evil is wrought from want of thought. If that young man
had possessed any sense he would have taken to his heels
and run the other way. But he had no power of resistance;
he was open and accessible:

A prudent man seeth evil and hideth himself,
but the simpletons pass on, and suffer for it.

(Proverbs 22:3)

He swallows everything he hears, so credulous is he and
simple:

The simpleton believes every word,
but the prudent man looks well to his going.

(Proverbs 14:15)

Nevertheless he is not beyond hope: if open to temptation,
he is also open to instruction:

Smite a scorner and the simpleton will learn prudence.

(Proverbs 19:25)

He is raw material, very raw, on which the sage can work,
just "a silly ass" who may yet become "a jolly good fellow."
Akin to this simpleton is another type mentioned ten
times in the book of Proverbs. He is the *Chaser leb*. This term
may be rendered into English by "Lack-brain," a term which
occurs in Shakespeare.[8] It may be that Shakespeare had this
character in mind. The Authorized Version renders this
phrase by "void of understanding," as in the passage just
quoted (Proverbs 7:7). Strictly it means "lacking heart":

[8]Henry IV, Part I.

Hebrew has no word for brain and the heart was the organ of intellection. Thus Lack-brain is a fairly precise rendering. This type is usually set in parallelism with *Pethi* as we have just seen, and will see again:

> Whoso is simple (*Pethi*) let him turn in hither,
> to him who is void of understanding (*Chaser leb*) she says,
> Come, eat my bread,
> drink the wine I have mixed.　　(Proverbs 9:4, cp. 9:16)

That is the invitation of Wisdom: in 7:7 the *Pethi* and the *Chaser leb* are set together as the harlot calls. The unreflecting simpleton may slide down the slippery slope and *Chaser leb* may injure mortally his manhood.

> He who commits adultery is a Lack-brain,
> He destroys himself who so acts.　　(Proverbs 6:32)

These two are just "plain dumb" and naïveté may land them in moral disaster. Their deficiency, however, can be corrected and if they listen to Wisdom they will be fortified.

> Folly is a delight to Lack-brain,
> But a man of understanding is straight in all his ways.
> 　　　　　　　　　　　　　　　　　(Proverbs 15:21)

Such a young man is apt to cause trouble and forget his social obligations:

> He who mocks his neighbor is a Lack-brain,
> But the discreet man holds his tongue.　　(Proverbs 11:12)

The faults here described are the sins and faults of youth, youth that does not think of what it is doing and has not yet comprehended the seriousness of life. The wise men had a chance with such material and they were assiduous in their calls to the young and in their endeavors to remedy defects that might become serious. A simpleton could be made

wise and Lack-brains could be filled with wisdom if the
sages caught them early enough. There was always present
the possibility that they might fall into wrong hands and
that the last state of these young men might be worse than
the first.

Another type of fool raises more serious problems. Two
different terms are used for this type: *Kĕsil* and *'ĕwil*, both
terms signifying a coarse and hardened fool, the second term
being slightly stronger than the first. They are the "swine"
who stop at no half-measures in their folly. They go "the
whole hog":

> As a dog returneth to his vomit,
> So doth a fool (*Kĕsil*) repeat his folly.   (Proverbs 26:11)

There is something beastly here. The simpleton is moved by
others but the *Kĕsil* and the *'ĕwil* move themselves and move
most energetically in the way of wickedness and folly. They
sin with "malice prepense" and Wisdom is anathema to them.

> It is a joke to a fool (*Kĕsil*) to act wickedly. (Proverbs 10:23)

Nor does he care a hoot who knows about his folly; he is
full of braggadocio:

> A sensible man conceals his folly,
> But fools (*Kĕsilim*) proclaim theirs.   (Proverbs 12:23)

Not content with this show of bravado this type of fool is
apt to become truculent and aggressive:

> An honor it is for man to keep from strife,
> But fools (*'ĕwilim*) will aye be brawling.   (Proverbs 20:3)

The sages had a hard time with those coarse-minded fools;
the teacher's job was no sinecure. Many a sore heart and

aching head did they cause to these wise men. The sages could do no mighty work there.

> A rebuke enters deeper into a man of sense
> Than a hundred stripes into a fool (*Kĕsil*). (Proverbs 17:10)

> Though thou shouldst bray a fool ('*ĕwil*) in a mortar
> Thou'lt not get his folly out of him. (Proverbs 27:22)

The sages often felt like kicking such fools but the fools kicked back and kicked hard. It is difficult to deal with thugs. Surely it is the voice of an exasperated sage we hear in these words:

> A whip for a horse, a bridle for an ass
> And a rod for the back of fools (*Kĕsilim*). (Proverbs 26:3)

Yet another type is represented by another term and this one presented the hardest problem of all to the sages. He is the *Letz*, the scorner. This type is objectionable both to men and God. There is something of the highbrow in him: his folly savors of arrogant superiority.

> The proud haughty man, scorner (*Letz*) is his name:
> He worketh in the arrogance of his pride. (Proverbs 21:24)

He is clever, devilishly clever, and full many a time did he cause the teacher to take a red face and slink away in confusion, for the *Letz* was a past master in the art of ribald interruption. The wise man could not descend to such a level and frequently the sages were left high and dry. It is not easy to answer a sneer and impossible to refute a miasmic atmosphere. If those gentle humanists ever used bad language it must have been towards the *Letzim*. Perhaps they just observed a profane silence!

But there is an ultimate decency of things, and those *Letzim* will get what is coming to them:

Judgments are prepared for scorners (*Letzim*),
and stripes for the back of fools (*Kĕsilim*).
(Proverbs 19:29)

These scorners filled no useful function for anyone. They
were a nuisance to society:

Cast out the *Letz* and contention will depart,
yea, strife and ignominy will cease.   (Proverbs 22:10)

Letzim set a city aflame,
But wise men turn away wrath.   (Proverbs 29:8)

They were hated of men, and God scoffs at them:

Surely He scorneth the scorners (*Letzim*)
but he giveth grace to the humble.   (Proverbs 3:34)

God himself pays them in their own coin: the verb used
of God's scorning is the verbal form of *Letz*.

Last of all in this melancholy descent comes the *Nabal*,
fool by name and fool by nature. He is the churl who calls
white black and black white. He inverts the scheme of moral
values. He it is who scorns the "god-idea" and says, "There
is no God" (Psalm 14:1).

Honest words do not become a Nabal.   (Proverbs 17:7)

He has a jaundiced soul and like *Nabal* (I Samuel 25:25)
he is totally lacking in ethical and spiritual perception. He
cannot see straight nor think straight: coarse-meated, coarse-
minded, he is near to the *Letz*—but worse.

"The fool," says G. K. Chesterton,

is one who has an impediment in his thought. It is not, as
modern fellows say, put there by his grandmother. I have
wandered over the world (so to speak) trying to find some
faithful, simple soul who really believed in his own grand-

mother. He does not exist. The first act of the fool, when he is articulate, is to teach his grandmother to suck eggs. Fools have no reverence. Fools have no humility.[9]

The sage's job was no picnic. It was uphill work.

> He that teaches a fool is as one that glueth a potsherd
>   together . . .
> He that discourseth to a fool is as one that discourseth
>   to a man asleep;
> At the end he will say, "What is it?"
>
> (Ecclesiasticus 22:7, 8)

How well we know that! We sometimes feel there is dry rot in the pulpit; here it seems to invade the pews:

> The mind of a fool is like a cartwheel,
>   and his thoughts like a rolling axle-tree.
>
> (Ecclesiasticus 33:5)

Like a hayseed blown by the east wind there he stands with mouth agape—the Fool.

> The eyes of a fool are in the ends of the earth.
>
> (Proverbs 17:24)

[9]Cited from **W. A. L. Elmslie,** *Studies in Life from Jewish Proverbs,* p. 132.

IV

Schools, Scribes and Sages

a) SCHOOLS AND TEACHERS

IT MAY NOT BE DENIED, therefore, that there was need of
Wisdom schools and Wisdom teachers. We need not be
surprised at the emergence of such schools and teachers.
Isaiah, Jeremiah, and Ezekiel are usually classified as seers
or prophets but they were more: they were religious educators, and that probably of necessity. For teaching must
accompany preaching if one would build up and edify a
group. Those educators were only too familiar with the products of the contemporary schools and they felt the need of
providing something better. Isaiah sets himself deliberately
to create such a school as will give adequate expression to
the prophetic ideals (Isaiah 8:16). Proverbs 25 represents
a collection of sayings made by the "men of Hezekiah" and
inasmuch as Hezekiah and Isaiah were on most friendly
terms and sought common goals it may well be that we have
here part of the prophet's religious instruction. Jeremiah
seems to have had a circle of disciples of whom Baruch is
best known, and it may be that the collection of Proverbs
22:17–24:22, made or copied in the days of Josiah, shows
the influence of Jeremiah.[1] In the Exile the Jews had ample
leisure and Ezekiel was a willing teacher. In Babylon the
Jewish Law was brought to its final form and a comprehen-

[1]Sellin, Ernst, *Israelitische-jüdische Religionsgeschichte* (1933), p. 114.

sive manual for religious instruction was found therein. In addition much of the ancient wisdom was assembled and shaped into literary form and a complete manual of instruction for youth was at hand. Here morality and religion, etiquette and general deportment were all taught on a religious basis.

> In one breath the sage will warn his pupil of unjust dealing before a partner or friend, of theft in the place where he sojourns, of falsifying an oath and a covenant, and of leaning on the table with his elbow when at meat.[2]

The production of career men was giving place to the ideal of character formation.

> Thus Wisdom was at first purely utilitarian and developed in course of time into a quality which was ethical and religious, while it continued to be used in the original sense as well. Ultimately it came to be identical with the Law.[3]

It may be noted that though the earlier teaching of the Sages was mainly prudential morality it was not without a religious basis. That basis may have been only a thin veneer. The scribes in Egypt were under the special care of the god Thoth as their patron deity and in Babylon the patron deity was Nebo, the divine scribe. Ahikar, who occupied a position of eminence in the government of Babylon, is referred to as "the wise and skilful scribe."[4]

In the Old Testament the class of Wise Men (*Chakamim*) seems to reach back and connect with the early government scribe (*Sopher*).[5] The town of Kirjath-sepher (booktown) is sometimes thought to have been a training center for

---

[2]W. A. L. Elmslie, *op. cit.*, p. 163.
[3]Oesterley & Robinson, *Introduction to the Old Testament* (1934), p. 156.
[4]A. Cowley, *Aramaic Papyri* (1923), p. 220.
[5]II Samuel 8:17, 20:25, I Kings 4:3, Jeremiah 36:20, 21.

scribes, but this is doubtful. The town seems to have been no more than a depot for the paper trade from Egypt as was Byblus in Phoenicia. That the scribe in Israel occupied a position similar to that of the scribes in Egypt and Babylon seems very probable. The fact that he occupied a high government position would constitute him a person of importance, a V. I. P.* His position, substance, and experience would well qualify him to give counsel, and it was counsel men sought from the sages.

The earliest reference to the Wise Men is in Isaiah 29:14 and it is not favorable:

> The wisdom of their wise men shall perish, and the understanding of their prudent men shall be hid.

Again in Jeremiah we find the Wise Men associated with the priest and prophet as popular leaders:

> The Law shall not perish from the priest, nor counsel from the wise, nor the word from the prophet. (Jeremiah 18:18)

In chapter 8:8 Jeremiah seems to identify scribe and sage:

> How say ye, we are wise, and the Law of the Lord is with us? Behold the false pen of the scribes hath wrought falsely.

Ecclesiasticus does not hesitate to apply both terms to himself although by his date the term scribe approaches more closely to the idea of one occupied with the letter and text of Scripture. That this idea came into vogue about the time of Ezra (400 B.C.) is a justifiable inference. At that date the sacred tongue, Hebrew, was becoming more and more unfamiliar to the common folk and interpreters were required to translate it into the popular Aramaic. It became the duty of the scribe to know the sacred text that he might expound it as "a ready scribe in the Law of Moses" (Ezra 7:6). Not

*Very important person.

only so, but he had to be familiar with the oral tradition that had developed: herein we observe the beginnings of the Talmud and the Rabbinate.

Oesterley thinks it must have been at a relatively early date, during the monarchy, that men from official circles concentrated on the study and collection of Wisdom material, "thus forming themselves into a distinct body, and becoming *Chăkamim* (Sages, Wise Men) in the technical sense of sages."[6] Not that we should think of this as the first attempt to create a Hebrew Academy. The growth may have been more gradual than Oesterley suggests. One could well imagine civil servants who had traveled abroad retiring to their homeland when their service was completed and willingly sharing their experience with those who sought to consult them. Such a person was well qualified to advise: he was experienced, mature, wise.

> He serveth among great men,
> And appeareth before a ruler:
> He traveleth in the land of foreign nations,
> And hath experience of both good and evil among men.
>
> (Ecclesiasticus 39:4)

The minds of such men had been enlarged by their travels and their sympathies had been liberalized through foreign contacts. They knew the best and the worst and they had a sense of values. Who might better train young men? And they trained youth on a broad cultural basis.

> The Wise Men represent the finest education of their period in combination with the pious spirit of their religion. It is an extraordinary feature of this Jewish scribism that it is not bound in national isolation and in narrow piety but that for its high leadership the most comprehensive viewpoint is not

[6]W. O. E. Oesterley, The Book of Proverbs (1929), p. 71.

too wide. These Sages have thus shared fully in the international exchange.[7]

This judgment applies to the period before Ezra but it must be modified for the later period.

b) RELATION OF SAGES TO PROPHETS AND PRIESTS

We have already indicated that in the earlier period the Sages did not find favor with the Prophets. Their wisdom savored too much of this world: it was of the earth, very earthy. They were too cold and unimpassioned for those ecstatic bearers of the prophetic word. Nonetheless, they are one with the prophets in that they find the service of God not in ritual devotion but in moral action, and with the great prophets they share the international viewpoint. But we can understand the attitude of the prophets: *the Sages reflected on the ways of God but the prophets knew God in living experience.*

The relation of the Sages to the priests seems to have been of a more friendly nature. This is easily understood. Both sage and priest regarded man as standing in a rational relationship to God and both held the same ideas as to the moral government of the world. The thought of divine recompense belongs to both Deuteronomy and Proverbs. "Prosperity is the blessing of the Old Testament"—both priest and sage act on that belief. Ultimately priest and sage arrive at the same place for they both hold a static view of revelation. And so it was that Wisdom is finally identified with the Jewish Law (*Torah*).

Though priests, prophets, and wise men are grouped together in Jeremiah 18:18 as leaders of the people, without

[7]Paul Volz, *Die Schriften des Alten Testament* (1921), Bd. III, Abt. 2, p. 113.

any sign of precedence to any particular group, the suc-
ceeding period saw the Sages become the most prominent
representatives of the people. The prophetic succession had
largely ceased and to the wise men and scribes fell the task
of interpreting the prophetic ideals. This they did in their
quiet unobtrusive way, mingling with people in their homes
and popular assemblies and winning for themselves a wel-
come which the more aloof prophets never knew. They carried their message into the homes of the people and button-
holed men on the street. They missed no opportunity. They
"sat where they sat" and by the solvent of sympathy and
mutual understanding they came closer to the common people and their needs than did their great inspired prophetic
predecessors. It is no exaggeration when Ranston says:

> It is customary, and with justification, to regard the prophets
> as the most illustrious exponents of the Hebrew religious
> spirit. But it may be doubted if the influence of these spiritual
> experts would have been so permanent and far-reaching
> apart from the work of the wise men in popularising their
> ideals and creating amongst the ordinary people a spirit sym-
> pathetic with them.[8]

The Sages were the spiritual middlemen who mediated the
exalted doctrines of the prophets and interpreted them in
terms of common life and experience. They succeeded where
the prophets failed: they reached the common people.

Moreover as a preparation for Christianity the work of
the Sages is of great significance. Though they do not deal
with the Messianic hope of Israel they revealed a broad
universalism and liberality of thought that largely prepared
the way for his coming. With them narrow bounds are tran-

---

[8] H. Ranston, *The Old Testament Wisdom Books and Their Teaching* (1930),
p. 19.

scended and the national is swallowed up in the international: Jew and Gentile are merged in the common idea of man. Here we have a *Praeparatio evangelica* of unique significance.

It is not obvious at first glance why the Sages should outstrip the priests in popular favor, but that they did so is beyond question. It is significant that in his *Praise of Famous Men* Ecclesiasticus[9] should omit Ezra and commemorate Nehemiah. Equally significant is the fact that the Wisdom Literature could develop as it did after Ezra's reformation and exaltation of the priesthood. It may be questioned whether the reforms of Ezra affected the life of the people as deeply as is suggested by the record.[10] After all it must be borne in mind that it was the priestly group who gave us the Old Testament in its present form and history can be written with a distinct bias.

The Priests suffered from certain necessary limitations. They were bound to, and fettered by, an institution. They occupied a hereditary office. As exponents of the Law they exercised a certain lordship over the people. The Sage, on the other hand, was something of a "free-lance," unfettered by any institutional ideas and able to express his own individuality. The profession, too, was open to all and sundry. Moreover, as already indicated, the Sage was usually a man of experience and often possessed an ample competence. These factors could not fail to impress the common people. The Sage, too, was peripatetic: he got around and moved about as he pleased. He could button-hole men in the street and speak with groups wherever he might find them. The priest waited for folk to come to the church, but in the Sage

9Ecclesiasticus, 44.
10E. Sellin, *op. cit.,* p. 116.

the church sought the people. This was a popular movement. Another reason for their popularity may have been
that they spoke of vital things in plain everyday speech.
They recognized that such an approach would appeal to
youth: young men are inclined to suspect pious talk. The
Sages knew how to get their man; there was nothing formal
in their approach.

The synagogue gave the Sages their opportunity. The life
of these synagogue assemblies was warm and less formal
than the stately temple services. In the temple ritual pre-
dominated, but in the synagogue the Word had a much
larger place and anyone with a message might be asked to
speak. There was a greater degree of liberty and in these
assemblies the Sages were often found. There is, however,
no trace of hostility or mutual jealousy between Priests and
Sages but rather a spirit of co-operation. There was more
affinity here than in the case of Sage and Prophet or Priest
and Prophet.

In the post-exilic period the Sages occupy a pre-eminent
place in the life of the nation. They were securely set in the
affections of the people and they became the real leaders.
They were not unconscious of their standing with the general public and the regarded their position with a high degree of pride. They seldom leave us in doubt as to their
sense of their own importance and although such a figure as
Elihu (Job 32:2 ff.) may seem almost comic to us he certainly did not so appear to his contemporaries. That same
bombastic style may still be heard in the Arabian desert as
may be seen from a modern example as given by Fulley-
love and Kelman:

> The elders sat silently leaning upon their staves except, now
> and then, when one of them would rise slowly and expatiate

upon something the sheikh had said—perhaps about camels or the grain-crop—beginning his interruption almost literally in the words of Job's friends: Hearken unto me, I also will give my opinion. I will answer; also, for my part, I also will show my opinion. For I am full of matter, the spirit within constraineth me.[11]

We need not attribute an undue superiority complex to the Hebrew. His natural language is hyperbole. The Sages knew, and they knew that they knew.

The golden age of the profession dates from 400–160 B.C. That is the heyday of the scribe and the sage. At the top stands Ezra "a ready scribe in the Law of Moses which the Lord God of Israel had given" (Ezra 7:6). At the other end stands the illustrious Jeshua ben Sirach, or Ecclesiasticus, conspicuous for his piety, his breadth of view, his culture, and his faith. Between these two we perceive a development of great importance. The earlier Sages had been mainly from the upper strata of society and were well-to-do men whose thought had been liberalized by travel and wide experience. Later, however, the Jewish passion for education—which is matched only by that of the Scot—reached to the lower levels of the population and the ranks of the profession were invaded by poor wise men who did not scorn to work at a trade and ply their wisdom-teaching on the side. The earlier group of Sages, understandably enough, had stood over against the working-classes as a distinct profession and often we can feel a touch of intellectual snobbery and sense the attitude that says, "I thank thee, Lord, that I am not as the butcher, the baker, and the candle-stick maker." This attitude can be observed in Ecclesiasticus though not in too pronounced degree:

[11]Fulleylove & Kelman, *The Holy Land*, pp. 103, 104 (cited from W. A. L. Elmslie, *op. cit.*, p. 57).

> The wisdom of the scribe cometh by opportunity of leisure,
> And he that hath little business shall become wise.
> How shall he become wise that guideth the plow,
> That glorieth in the shaft of the goad,
> That driveth oxen, and is busied with their labors,
> And whose discourse is of the stock of bulls?   (38:24, 25)

This may savor somewhat of the aristocratic Horace[12] and
his *Odi profanum vulgus et arceo* (I hate the common herd
and repel them), or it may suggest the attitude of the cul-
tured Greek towards the *hoi polloi* (the masses). At best
there is a kindly tolerance perhaps mingled with a thinly
veiled contempt. The later rabbis did not follow Ecclesiasticus in this way of thinking but they did esteem some
trades better than others. Ass-drivers were looked upon as
rather a low lot, presumably because the ass and the mule
have the capacity to provoke variegated language of a profane type. Camel-drivers were rated higher, and sailors, then
as now, were credited with considerable piety. The best of
physicians was only fit for Gehenna while the butcher was
a bloody-minded man, a son of Amalek. Tanners, weavers,
and hairdressers enjoyed no high repute. It might be easy
for the son of Sirach to adopt this attitude for he was born
"with a silver spoon in his mouth," but most of the rabbis
had to "work their way through college." And the Talmud
urges work of this kind:

> Whoso doth not teach his son to work teaches him to steal.[13]

About 90 A.D. we have the expressed judgment of Gamaliel:

> An excellent thing is study of the Law combined with some
> worldly trade . . . but all study of the Law apart from manual
> toil must fail at last, and be the cause of sin.[14]

Another puts it more forcibly:

[12]Horace, *Odes,* III, 1.   [13]Kiddushin 99a.   [14]Aboth 2:1 f.

> Flay a carcass in the street and earn a living, and say not,
> I am a famous man, and such work is beneath my dignity.[15]

Paul is a standing type of the later Jewish rabbi and he learned his trade as a tentmaker.

> Some of the best known rabbis of the Middle Ages supported themselves by laboring as carpenters, shoemakers, builders, bakers, and so forth.[16]

It is not difficult to trace the consequences of this development which began probably in the Greek period (after 333 B.C.). A less liberal group began to appear and there is a notable contraction of sympathy and interest. The wide opportunities of travel that were the lot of earlier Sages were not open to these "homekeeping wits." Simultaneously with the rise of Greek influence Israel was forced to act on the defensive and she withdrew more and more within herself. There is a distinct narrowing of intellectual interest. National exclusiveness was accentuated and the sectarian spirit grew apace. This can be observed most clearly in Ecclesiasticus where Wisdom is now equated with the Jewish Law and Wisdom is regarded as God's gift to Israel:

> Let thy converse be with the man of understanding,
> and let all thy discourse be in the Law of the Most High.
> (9:15)

Zion became the abode of Wisdom and "salvation is of the Jews" (Ecclesiasticus 24:10–12). Thus interest was narrowed and became centered on the letter to the exclusion of the spirit. The Talmud begins to take form and the unlovely form of the New Testament scribe begins to emerge before our eyes.

[15]Pesachim 113a.
[16]W. A. L. Elmslie, *op. cit.*, p. 119.

c) THE TEACHING OF THE SAGES

It is not intended here to give the whole body of instruction offered by the Sages but rather to indicate its general outline. Before we proceed to set this forth let us consider the form and structure of the Book of Proverbs wherein is contained most of the teaching of the Sages.

d) THE BOOK OF PROVERBS

The present writer can only think of this book with a large measure of affection for it has always been the favorite book of Scotsmen: probably no other book of the Bible has had a more lasting influence on the character of that people. John Ruskin loved that book above all others and we would venture to say that it had much to do with the foundation of the British Empire, for those early pioneers were men who had imbibed the teaching of this book from their earliest years. It entered into the fiber of character.

The Book of Proverbs, as might be inferred from what we have already said regarding the growth and development of Hebrew Wisdom, represents the garnered wisdom of many centuries and it contains the distilled essence of the thought of countless generations. Here we have a compilation of separate collections and these separate collections are not difficult to discern: several of them bear titles on their heads.

The first section (1:1–9:18) bears the general title. "The Proverbs of Solomon, the son of David, king of Israel." It is the most philosophical and theological section and is notable for its personalization of Wisdom (8:1; also 1:20–23, 9:1–6). Quite obviously such advanced ideas could not originate in the earlier periods of Hebrew history and most scholars are agreed that this is the latest section in the book and that it cannot be dated earlier than about 250 B.C.

The second section (10:1—22:16) bears the title, "The Proverbs of Solomon" and contains 375 sayings: the number 375 is the precise numerical equivalent of the Hebrew letters forming the name Solomon. This section shows signs of greater antiquity and is probably the oldest part of the book. The first section (1:1—9:18) is formed of a group of short essays, a structure similar to that found in Ecclesiasticus, but in this second and older section we find mainly self-contained couplets and occasionally single-lined sayings of the earliest type of *Mashal*. Chapters 10–15 employ usually antithetic parallelism[17] while in chapters 16–22 the parallelism is usually of synonymous or continuous form. Doublets—that is, the same saying repeated twice—occur not only between these two groups but within each group. Oesterley would date this second section not later than 700 B.C. and it may contain material that is much older.

The third section, "Sayings of the Wise" (22:17—24:34), may be divided into three smaller sub-sections. Such is the opinion of Oesterley but for our general purpose we treat it as a whole. Here again there is a difference in form, for while the sayings of 10—22:16 are set forth in couplets and simply recorded here we have quatrains and the sayings are addressed to the hearer. In this section, too, we find part of the teaching of Amen-em-ope incorporated (22:17—23:14). Here we see once more the cosmopolitan character of Wis-

---

[17]Hebrew poetry does not employ rhyme (though there are rare exceptions to this). Instead of rhyme we find a recurrence of thought rather than recurrence of sound. One line is balanced with another either by identity or by contrast of thought. The former is called Synonymous Parallelism while the latter is named Antithetic Parallelism. Synonymous Parallelism may be illustrated by Proverbs 16:15:

> In the light of the king's countenance is life:
> And his favour is as a cloud of the latter rain.

Antithetic Parallelism may be illustrated by Proverbs 14:5:

> A faithful witness will not lie:
> But a false witness will utter lies.

dom. These sections Oesterley would assign to the seventh century B.C. while Pfeiffer would date it in the post-exilic period.

The fourth section (25–29) is dated by Oesterley and Sellin in the age of Hezekiah. It bears the inscription, "These also are proverbs of Solomon which the men of Hezekiah, King of Judah, copied out." The words "copied out" in this expression would seem to indicate a late period as the Hebrew word here is not used in this sense before the Rabbinical period. Eissfeldt judges Oesterley's date not impossible, but the writer feels it is post-exilic.

The fifth section (30:1–14) is entitled "the words of Agur, son of Jakeh, of Massa." This seems to point to an Arabian point of origin, as does also "the words of King Lemuel" (31:1–9; sixth section). The seventh section, 30:15–33 is without identification, while 31:10–31 contains a poem in praise of the Virtuous Woman (eighth section). To none of these sections can we assign a date. These last four sections occupy a different position in the Greek Bible (LXX) and clearly appear to be later additions to the book.

Thus we may judge that the book is a post-exilic production, but it contained, like the Law and the Psalter, much ancient material.

e) NATURE AND CONTENT OF THE TEACHING

We now come to look at what the book contained and hear what the Sages had to say. This teaching is characterized by a breadth of human interest: these Hebrew Humanists count nothing alien to them. Their parish is the world.

> Unto you, O men, I call,
> And my voice is unto the sons of men.   (Proverbs 8:4)

This is as near as the Hebrew could come to the thought

of what we call "humanity." Wisdom addresses man as man: its appeal is not to Jew or Gentile but to Everyman. Thus it is at home in Edom (Jeremiah 49:7) and in Egypt (Genesis 41:8): it has its abode in Tyre (Ezekiel 28:2) and it is no stranger in Babylon (Jeremiah 50:35, 51:57). Nor is Persia outside its range (Esther 1:13, 6:13). Wisdom is the true cosmopolitan and it is international in character. For this reason there is little or no mention of Jewish ritual, of Jerusalem, or of Messiah: all these are local or national concerns which Wisdom transcends. Humanity is the subject of study. These Humanists were of the opinion that "the proper study of mankind is man."

The teaching is marked by a healthy optimism and even expressed in terms of worldliness. They are more interested in feasting than in fasting. There is little of what we call other-worldliness here. Even Ecclesiastes, for all his gloom, cannot suppress the prevailing mood: even with "the gloomy dean" cheerfulness is always breaking forth.

> Go, eat in Cheerfulness thy daily Food,
> and drink thy Wine as an Immortal should,
> be well content, while yet thou canst enjoy,
> that God is pleased to let thee still see Good.

> Put off thy Mourning, give the rein to Mirth,
> cherish thy wife while yet thou art on Earth,
> while yet the Bubble lasts under the Sun—
> this is what God has judged thy Toil is worth.[18]

There is throughout a sheer *joie de vivre* which even the gloomy Qoheleth cannot hide. Proverbs, too, knows it well:

> The light of the eyes rejoiceth the heart,
> and good tidings maketh the bones fat.
>
> (Proverbs 15:30)

[18]Ecclesiastes 9:7–9, translated by F. C. Burkitt (1922).

Robert Browning knows it well as he writes in *Saul:*

> How good is man's life, the mere living! how fit to employ
> all the heart and the soul and the senses forever in joy.

The Hebrew looked on the bright side of things: he was an incorrigible optimist:

> The glory of young men is their strength,
> and the beauty of old men is the hoary head.
> (Proverbs 20:29)

Man was created for the good—and the goods!

> Love not sleep, lest thou come to poverty.
> Open thine eyes and thou shalt have bread aplenty.
> (Proverbs 20:13)

Earthly possessions have value and they are worthy of a man's main effort:

> In all labor there is profit,
> but mere talk leadeth to poverty. (Proverbs 14:23)

Life, moreover, is beset with pitfalls, but a man does not need to be a fool:

> My son, if sinners entice thee,
> consent thou not. (Proverbs 1:10)

> Eat thou not the bread of him that hath an evil eye,
> neither desire thou his dainties. (Proverbs 23:6)

"God's in his heaven"—though that is not overemphasized —"all's right with the world." (Browning.)

> The blessing of the Lord, it maketh rich,
> and he addeth no sorrow with it. (Proverbs 10:22)

Verily it shall be well with the righteous, and to be righteous is to be wise:

The fear of the Lord is the foundation of wisdom:
wisdom and discipline fools despise.   (Proverbs 1:7)

There is no thought of future judgment or of the kingdom
of God but the world is moral at bottom and man will not
fail of his due reward:

He who gives heed to the word will prosper,
and whoso trusteth in the Lord, happy is he.
(Proverbs 16:20)

The Sages, of course, do not shoot at the moon. They are
marked by moderation. They do not look for supermen, but
if they can subtract from the number of fools and add to
the number of the wise they will not have labored in vain.
Their aim is one possible of attainment. No heroic ideals are
here, only sanctified common-sense, moderation, temperance,
self-control. These find response from men as the loftier and
more inaccessible ideas and ideals of the prophets never did.
Cautions against over-sleeping, over-eating, over-drinking
abound in this teaching. Immoderate anger and hasty speech
are alike condemned:

He that guardeth his mouth keepeth his life,
but he that openeth wide his lips shall be destroyed.
(Proverbs 13:3)

"Shut mouths catch no flies," say the Scots, and the Sages
felt that way also. The wise man will not give way to passion:

He that is slow to anger is better than the mighty,
and he who rules his spirit than he who takes a city.
(Proverbs 16:32)

This is certainly a far remove from the prophetic spirit. The seers of Israel were active and energetic but with the Sages the passive virtues are more in demand. Social passion is conspicuous by its absence. In this respect the Wisdom Literature stands lower than Deuteronomy and is very far removed from the New Testament. The "policy of the good neighbor" is not here. After all, the wise man will mind his own business. Nobody needs to be a fool, and a meddler will get little for his pains:

> He seizeth a dog by the ears
> who meddles with a quarrel not his own.   (Proverbs 26:17)

Thus the negative side of things gets greater emphasis than the positive:

> To depart from evil, that is wisdom.   (Job 28:28)

The appeal to self-interest is prominent and the motives here are self-regarding. Probably the Semite could not help that, for thousands of years in the desert necessarily made him so: the desert was cruel and men had to develop a strong self-regarding instinct to survive. But the Old Testament reveals a higher level than is found elsewhere and there is an advancing sentiment in the Wisdom Literature. "The good name that is better than precious ointment," the applause and approval of one's fellowmen are highly prized:

> The crucible is for silver, the furnace for gold,
> and a man is to be estimated according to his reputation.
>   (Proverbs 27:21)

The consciousness of personal integrity takes high rank among the goods of life:

> Better is little with righteousness
> than great revenues with injustice.   (Proverbs 16:8)

Better a poor man whose life is straight
than one whose conduct is base, though he is rich.

(Proverbs 28:6)

The thought of moral responsibility begins to find expression and the sense of social obligation comes into view:

For from a man of understanding shall a city be peopled, but by a race of wicked men it shall be desolate.

(Ecclesiasticus 16:4)

There is no conception of absolute moral law: the central interest is egotistic and negative:

Do no evil, so shall no evil overtake thee:
Depart from wrong, and it shall turn away from thee.

(Ecclesiasticus 7:1)

Men had to wait until Jesus Christ came with the emancipating word, "Whatsoever ye would that men should do to you, do ye even so to them" (Matthew 7:12). The fulness of time was not yet come. The ideal of the Sages is that a man should mind his own business and not interfere with other folks' affairs. It is frankly self-regarding and eudaemonistic.

All this means, in large measure, an absence of idealism. Nothing could be further removed from the prophetic attitude. Nevertheless, the Book of Proverbs would never have found such a place in the life of men, particularly Scotsmen, unless it possessed elements of real value. The Sages were practical, realists: the prophets were visionaries, idealists. Where the prophets called the people could seldom follow but the Wise men entered into the common life of common folk and imbued that life with uncommon moral earnestness, integrity, and truth. They made the prophetic ideals real and that is no mean service. Their close connection with human beings and their human concerns achieved more than the comparative aloofness of the prophets who stood in the "council of the Almighty." Without the Sages the prophetic ideals would not have found lodgment in the popular mind. The solvent of the Sages' sympathy wrought most wonderfully.

f) WHAT IS WISDOM?

Perhaps we may look back here for a moment and see what we have garnered. Wisdom in the eyes of the Sages was both the fundamental principle of the universe and the guide of human life. This was a feature common to Wisdom Literature generally. Laotse's philosophy of the universe and his doctrinal instruction center around Tao, a supernatural form of universal significance which possesses absolute truth, being, and goodness. The true man is he who is complete in Wisdom. Likewise in Greece the wise man is the ideal both in the time of Solon and in the later period. Wisdom is exalted to a position of distinction that can be understood only as we recall that originally she was a deity—Ea in Babylon, Athena in Greece, and later Isis in the Egypto-Hellenic world. Something of this mythology may appear in the Old Testament, particularly in Proverbs, chapter 7, where, according to Rankin, we have Iranian influence.[19] But monotheism spells death to all such mythology and such an idea could not survive in Judaism. The conception was anathema to Ecclesiasticus and it is not found outside the latest section of the Book of Proverbs (1–9). The Sages saw Wisdom in Creation and Providence: it is the underlying principle of the universe as it is of human life. To have Wisdom and to walk by it is to be in harmony with the Creator.

[19]O. S. Rankin, *Israel's Wisdom Literature* (1936), pp. 223–264.

It signifies the building of life on the principle that informs and sustains the universe.

The Hebrew could not advance beyond that point. The speculative instinct that would naturally issue in philosophy is not found here—with the partial exception of Ecclesiastes—though it found free course in India and the Greek world. The Hebrew was practical and conduct was his main interest—right conduct, piety. He believed in walk rather than talk. Thus he came straight to the position that Wisdom is morality and religion: "The fear of the Lord is the foundation of wisdom." That verse occurs again and again, and "the fear of the Lord" is just a Hebrew synonym for religion. This wisdom has been revealed in their history, and the record is plain for all to see and read—the Law, the Prophets, and the Writings. Doubtless, as we have observed in the foregoing pages, there was danger of narrowness and limitation which, though not at first apparent, became clear in the later Sages and emerges into fuller light in the pages of the New Testament.

We shall next proceed to examine how those Hebrew Sages dealt with the deeper problems of human life and consider their attitude to the *Problem of Pain and Evil.*

V

The Ways of God with Men

THUS FAR WE HAVE BEEN considering the sayings of the Wise and we have observed how those sayings are concerned with the business of living. They are of a prudential and utilitarian character and not unlike such precepts found elsewhere in the ancient world. We could parallel most of these sayings with similar teachings from Marcus Aurelius in Rome or Epictetus in Greece; we could also hear the voice of these Sages in Alexander Pope in England or Benjamin Franklin in America, though in these cases the voice might seem but an echo. Perhaps this teaching of the Sages was inevitable when the Hebrew view was limited to the things of space and time and life itself was rather circumscribed. For the thought of life hereafter had not yet entered men's minds to any large extent. The horizon was close and man had to work while it was day, for the night must come when man would work no more. And so men sought to make the most of time while it was theirs and to do with all their might whatever their hand might find to do. The Sages with their pithy maxims sought to aid men so to live that the clean things might not lose their cleanness nor the bright things their brightness. It was a simple philosophy that taught men to do and to do without and finally to depart.

a) THE BEGINNINGS OF SPECULATION

With the passage of time and the growing complexity of life there came deeper insight into the meaning of life and a fuller knowledge of God and His purpose. There was growth and development, and enquiring minds interrogated accepted ideas in the light of experience. *Experientia docet:* life itself becomes our teacher. Areas of truth hitherto unknown were revealed and human thought and action combined to disclose problems hitherto unsuspected. Books like Job and Ecclesiastes come not at the beginning of an era but at its end. They are the products of maturity.

Thus eventually the Sages came to deal with the greater issues and the larger problems that lie not out on the periphery of life but at its very center. And the main problem here is the problem of *Human Suffering and Pain.*

This problem only emerges in presence of a theistic faith and indeed it constitutes the main problem for such faith. Where there is no belief in a good God the problem will not arise. Even in a theistic system it need not necessarily arise. Islam is a monotheistic faith but in Islam the idea of divine sovereignty is so strongly emphasized that the problem of innocent suffering does not really emerge. Whatever Allah wills is right and none will question that sovereign will. *Kama yesha* (as He wills) is a constantly recurring phrase in the Koran and all discussion of difficult problems is closed off and banned with the words *Allah akbar* (God is great). The present writer was born and reared in a strict Calvinistic atmosphere and has seen Calvinism work frequently to produce a dumb resignation not unlike that of the Moslem. There may be a degree of truth in Dean Inge's saying that "Calvinism is just Stoicism baptised" though there may not be as much truth in that as he thinks. It may be worth noting here in passing how our Lord acted in this respect. He prayed "Let this cup pass from me"—for no man seeks suffering for its own sake—and only when he saw clearly that it was the will of the Father did he say, "Nevertheless, not my will but thine be done." From this we might justifiably infer that there is a place for resignation in the religious life but it is not the first place. Resignation is the last word in religion.

b) THE PROPHETIC FAITH

Here it will reward us to look back a little and consider how this problem forced itself upon men's minds in the later stages of the Old Testament. Only thus can we understand how the Book of Job came to be written.

The development stems from the prophetic faith and from the Prophet's idea of God. It may have been implicit in the early faith of the Hebrews but it was the Prophets who unfolded it and made it explicit. Amos in the eighth century B.C. presents us with the thought of a God who is not one among many but is the only God, Lord of Nature and Lord of History. He made and controls the world and all that is therein. He guides the movements of the nations and He it is who calls the Philistines from the midland sea and the Syrians from Kir: the men in far-off Ethiopia are subject to His call and disposing (Amos 9:7). All these are under His control and they move according to His purpose; they are the instruments in His hand. Assyria is "the rod of mine anger, and the staff in their hand is mine indignation" (Isaiah 10:5). The day was now gone by when men could explain their suffering and ill-fortune by ascribing them to the greater might and malevolence of another god. Israelites may not

say any more that their defeat by Moab was due to the wrath
of Chemosh (II Kings 3:27) or the Syrians might attribute
their reverse at the hands of Israel to the fact that Yahwe
was "a god of the hills" (I Kings 20:23). No limit can be
set to the power and reach of Israel's God. Men might evade
the greater issues of life by their limited thought of the
divine power but that was no longer possible when the
prophets set forth Yahwe as the one almighty God and declared human history to be the vehicle of His revelation.

Nor was it only power that was revealed here. The moral
character of God was clearly declared. Not only in the charge
against Israel, to whom much had been given and from whom
much was required (Amos 3:2), but in the oracles against
the nations who had broken the fundamental law of humanity engraved on the heart and conscience of every human
being (Amos 1 and 2), did Amos reveal the wrath of God
against all iniquity and show Him to be of purer eyes than
to look on any unclean thing (cp. Habakkuk 1:13). God
was infinitely great and absolutely pure. He was altogether
righteous and justice was His demand. Thus the prophet can
sum up His teaching in two words:

Seek the Lord and ye shall live.   (Amos 5:6)
Seek good and not evil, that ye may live.   (Amos 5:14)

And Micah will sum it all up in his memorable word:

What doth the Lord require of thee, but to do justly, and
to love mercy, and to walk humbly with thy God?
(Micah 6:8)

"The theology of the Old Testament is, to a very large
extent, Theodicy, the justification of the ways of God with
men." So writes the late D. S. Cairns,[1] of beloved memory,

[1] D. S. Cairns, *The Riddle of the World* (1937), p. 230.

and rightly so. For the prevailing cry of the Old Testament is just "My God, my God, why?" or yet again, "How long, O Lord, how long?" For men are pained with the pressure of life and seek an answer to the riddle of life. Life must be interpreted in the light of divine purpose.

c) THE PROBLEM OF SUFFERING

If this world is ruled and directed by a just and righteous God, why do men suffer? Is not suffering a moral anomaly in such a world? And yet none then, as now, could dispute the fact of pain and evil. The Hebrews sought to explain this and the first thing they said was that suffering is to be explained in terms of *Retribution*. That is the main word of the Old Testament though there are other suggestions which will be considered in the course of our discussion. This principle is manifest in the Book of Job as throughout the whole Old Testament; it is very manifest in the Book of Deuteronomy under whose influence the whole early history of the Hebrews was edited and interpreted to show the validity of this idea. Our Lord seems to apply this very same principle when he tells the story of the house built on rock and contrasts its fate with that of the house built on sand (Matthew 7:24–27). Paul does not go beyond it when he says:

> For we must all appear before the judgment seat of Christ: that every one may receive the things *done* in *his* body according to that he hath done, whether it be good or bad.
>
> (II Corinthians 5:10)

There is indeed ample reason for Lord Bacon's oft quoted word, "Prosperity is the blessing of the Old Testament." Throughout the Old Testament there is a close connection between piety and prosperity: our study of the Book of Job will clearly demonstrate that fact.

There was a man in the land of Uz, whose name was Job; and that man was perfect and upright, one that feared God and eschewed evil. And there were born unto him seven sons and three daughters. His substance also was seven thousand sheep, and three thousand camels, and five hundred yoke of oxen, and five hundred she-asses, and a very great household; so that this man was the greatest of all the men of the east.   (Job 1:1–3)

That is as it should be and the Hebrew could not conceive of it being otherwise. That is the law of God written into the constitution of the universe, or rather that is what they thought in that early time. Nor is this peculiar to Job: everywhere throughout the Old Testament we find prosperity regarded as the inevitable accompaniment of piety. We find the idea set right at the beginning of the Psalter:

> That man hath perfect blessedness
> who walketh not astray
> In counsel of ungodly men
> nor stands in sinners' way,
> Nor sitteth in the scorner's chair:
> But placeth his delight
> Upon God's law, and meditates
> on his law day and night.

> He shall be like a tree that grows
> near planted by a river,
> Which in his season yields his fruit,
> And his leaf fadeth never:
> And all he doth shall prosper well.
> The wicked are not so;
> But like they are unto the chaff
> which wind drives too and fro.

> In judgment therefore shall not stand
> such as ungodly are;
> Nor in th'assembly of the just

> shall wicked men appear.
> For why? the way of godly men
> unto the Lord is known:
> Whereas the way of wicked men
> shall quite be overthrown.
>
> (Psalm 1: *Metrical Version*)

The post-exilic prophet Haggai brings this idea to encourage a people laggard in its religious service:

> Ye looked for much, and, lo, *it came* to little; and when ye brought it home I did blow upon it. Why? Because of mine house that *is* waste, and ye run every man unto his own house.
>
> (Haggai 1:9)

Malachi does not fail to stress it in similar circumstances:

> Bring ye all the tithes into the storehouse . . . and prove me now herewith, saith the Lord of hosts, if I will not open you the windows of heaven, and pour you out a blessing, that *there shall* not *be room* enough *to receive it.*
>
> (Malachi 3:10)

These writers leave us in no doubt as to their fundamental belief that piety ensures prosperity. Righteous conduct is sure of its reward. Religion pays dividends. The Adversary plainly understood that when he asked, "Doth Job serve God for nought?" There were dangers latent in this way of thinking as we shall see presently.

But there is more here than is apparent at first glance. In a sense this was a logical belief. For the Hebrew began with a fundamental faith in the righteousness of God. "Shall not the Judge of all the earth do right?" (Genesis 18:25). Moreover in the Old Testament the hope of life hereafter does not appear until very late. Thus the Hebrew judged that in a world ruled by a righteous God there can be no moral anomalies. If a righteous God is on the throne then man's inward character and his outward circumstance must correspond. Prosperity must accompany piety. And on the smaller scale of tribal life things might well work that way: the man of approved character would come to the top and wealth, and honor would be his portion. Such exceptions as occurred would only prove the rule.

But there is danger in such a belief and time soon made that very clear. For if we say that prosperity is the sign of piety then we cannot evade the corollary of such a proposition and say that suffering and pain are the signs of sin. And that is precisely what men did say. One has only to read the record to see the common attitude to suffering in the Old Testament. The Psalmist tells us of his sickness and how "mine own familiar friend . . . hath lifted up his heel against me" (Psalm 41:9). Suffering and sickness alienated erstwhile friends and relations. Their religious faith compelled them to taunt the sufferer with bitter chiding words, "Where is thy God?" (Psalm 42:3). And why not? For poverty, pain, and suffering were not simply crude facts: they were the sign and seal of a righteous judgment from a righteous God. At the very point where man most needed God he was regarded as cut off from him. For that reason we do not find in the Old Testament any glorification of monasticism or the ascetic life; these may be found elsewhere but they are not found in Israel. There is no Gospel for the poor in the Old Testament. There is but one judgment on poverty and suffering:

"We did esteem him stricken, smitten of God, and afflicted."
(Isaiah 53:4)

The poor sufferer did not have a chance: his character was slain with a logical syllogism. "All Sufferers are Sinners." Job's friends were theologically sound though they were miserable comforters.

Old theologies never die. They linger on and seem to be endowed with perennial youth. We find this same attitude in the New Testament:

> Master, who did sin, this man or his parents, that he was born blind?   (John 9:2)

The disciples were children of their time and they could not think of suffering without thinking of sin as its cause. Nor is it otherwise today as any observant pastor will testify. Progressive revelation progresses slowly, very slowly.

We may pause here to trace the development that came in the process of time. For theology must always deal with the facts of life and deal with them adequately. Choice spirits arose who discerned the inadequacy of the current theology and when men saw a life like that of Jeremiah, so full of passion, power, and godlikeness, they refused to say any more "*All Sufferers are Sinners.*" Men could not look on the saintly impassioned man of Anathoth and think to comprehend such a life as that in a cliché phrase. As they marked the vast expense of spirit and travail of soul in the prophet laboring for the redemption of "my people" they modified the old phrase and they came to say, "*Some Sufferers are Saints.*" That was an advance forced upon such discerning spirits by experience, though such an advance was only shared by few. Later still when men saw the Suffering Servant of Isaiah 53, men felt still another advance must be made if theology was to be true to life. The change was not easily made, but we see how it came about.

> He is despised and rejected of men; a man of sorrows, and acquainted with grief: and we hid as it were our faces from him; he was despised and we esteemed him not.
>
> (Isaiah 53:3)

But it is not possible for the eye forever to cheat the conscience and the deeper truth may not forever be resisted.
They looked again and they saw it was for sin he suffered
—*but it was not his sin.*

> Surely he hath borne our griefs, and carried our sorrows:
> yet we did esteem him stricken, smitten of God, and afflicted.
> But he was wounded for our transgressions, he was bruised
> for our iniquities: the chastisement of our peace was upon
> him; and with his stripes we are healed.   (Isaiah 53:4, 5)

In view of that wonderful figure they could not rest where
once they rested and they moved on to say, "*Some Sufferers
are Saviors.*" Beyond this the Old Testament does not advance and beyond this single reference there is no view of
vicarious suffering in the Old Testament.

One has the feeling at times that these Old Testament
saints often spoke bigger words than they thought. And that
may well be the case here: it was left for later generations
to interpret this experience and the word concerning it.

The question concerning the Suffering Servant is notori-
ously difficult and countless volumes have been written on
the subject. And men still ask with the Ethiopian eunuch,

> I pray thee, of whom speaketh the prophet this? of himself,
> or of some other man?   (Acts 8:34)

The Christian Church had an answer to that question. To
whom could it refer more suitably than to our Lord Jesus
Christ? For the unique thing about suffering in Isaiah 53 is
the reaction of the Sufferer. "He opened not his mouth." In
every other instance of suffering in the Old Testament we
have one of two reactions: either the sufferer will confess his
sin and seek the forgiveness of God and the restoration of
his salvation (Psalm 51) or he will speak in tones of defiance

and challenge the justice of God (the Book of Job). But in this present instance we have something unique: silence in the presence of suffering. Men had never seen it in that fashion before. And that is why the Christian Church interpreted the passage on the Suffering Servant with reference to Jesus. For no one ever heard him express doubt as to the character of the Father and though he taught others to confess sin he never had to do so himself. Surely the Church was rightly guided in this interpretation for in Christ alone do we find vicarious suffering of redemptive avail in universal degree. For the whole world "has rest by His sorrow and life by His death."

So much it has been necessary to say by way of introduction to the Book of Job, and with this in mind we may now proceed to a closer examination of that masterpiece of Hebrew life and literature.

VI

The Book of Job

In the Book of Job we have the finest masterpiece of the
Hebrew literary genius. Here we have a work second to none
in the whole range of world literature. Here a daring, rich,
and original mind deals with a universal element of human
life and deals with it in a high and solemn manner. The
author lived long, long ago in the rock-ribbed desert beside
the thunder-riven hills and his story is set in an ancient setting and written in an ancient language, but by its nobility
and power and truth it transcends all such limitations of
space and time and speaks home to the heart of Everyman.
We deal here with something elemental and fundamental:
"deep calleth unto deep." Here is a true book for it is written
with the lifeblood of a man: it speaks the language of the
heart—the broken heart—and that is language that Everyman can understand.

a) LITERARY APPRECIATIONS

It matters not how we classify this book—epic, drama, or
didactic poem. It overtops all our narrow and neat formulae:
it is unique, it is *sui generis*—it is itself. Its intellectual courage, its psychological insight, and its brilliant glowing imagery thrill us with an emotion like that of stout Cortez

> when with eagle eyes
> He stared at the Pacific, and all his men
> Look'd at each other with a wild surmise,
> Silent, upon a peak in Darien.
>
> (Keats, "Chapman's Homer")

This view of the book is confirmed by a look at the various estimates made by great literary critics. These will be found in most commentaries on the book and for those that follow here we are indebted to the excellent commentary of James Strahan.[1] This commentary and that of A. S. Peake (in the *Century Bible* series) are about the best helps an English reader can lay hands upon. The Book of Job is not easily understood without the aid of a good commentary.

Let us hear J. G. von Herder, philosopher and theologian, whose most notable work, *Vom Geist der hebräischen Poesie*, was translated into English in 1833 under the title *The Spirit of Hebrew Poetry:*

> "Its way of thinking is majestic and divine: it gives and will for ever give reviving energy to the faint and strength to the powerless."[2]

Bishop Lowth, who did much to pioneer studies in Hebrew Poetry, held that "it stands single and unparalleled in the sacred volume"[3] while Renan judged it to be

> "the Hebrew book *par excellence*. . . . It is in the Book of Job that the force, the beauty, the depth of the Hebrew genius are seen at their best."[4]

A. B. Davidson spoke of it as "the most splendid creation of Hebrew poetry," while A. M. Fairbairn described it in these terms:

[1] James Strahan, *The Book of Job*, Second Edition (1914)
[2] J. G. von Herder, *Vom Geist der hebräischen Poesie I*, p. 143.
[3] R. Lowth, *Lectures on Hebrew Poetry* (1839), p. 353.
[4] E. Renan, *History of the People of Israel*, III, pp. 65, 71

"the highest achievement of the Hebrew, or rather of the Semitic spirit, the ripe and fragrant fruit not so much of a man's or a people's genius as of the genius of a race."[5]

And if one may add a third Scot to the foregoing two it will be the testimony of one who was little disposed to bestow bouquets at any time. Here Thomas Carlyle waxes lyrical:

> I call it, apart from all theories about it, one of the grandest things ever written with pen. One feels, indeed, as if it were not Hebrew: such a noble universality, different from noble patriotism or noble sectarianism, reigns in it. A noble book: all men's book! It is our first, oldest statement of the never-ending problem—man's destiny and God's way with him here on this earth. And all in such free flowing outlines; grand in its sincerity, in its simplicity; in its epic melody and repose of reconcilement. . . . Sublime sorrow, sublime reconciliation; oldest, choral melody as of the heart of mankind;—so soft and great; as the summer midnight, as the world with its seas and stars! There is nothing written, I think, in the Bible or out of it, of equal literary merit.[6]

Few will disagree with the Sage of Chelsea. But let this be said in addition: Job is not easy to read and if we would follow the progress of the dialogue we must have the Revised Version in our hands or some one of the modern translations. Job will not yield his secret easily, but our labor and our earnest quest will not fail of rich reward.

The book is partly in prose and partly poetical. Chapters I and II form the Prologue while the Epilogue is found in Chapter 42:7–17. Between these two lies the Poem of Job. The author of the prose parts is not the author of the Poem. The Prologue and the Epilogue are the remains of an earlier popular tale which told of the sufferings of the righteous

[5]A. M. Fairbairn, *The City of God*, p. 143.
[6]Carlyle, Thomas, *Lectures on Heroes* ("The Hero as Prophet").

Job and how his friends advised him, as did Job's own wife, to blaspheme God. "They did not speak the thing that is right, as [did] my servant Job" (Job 42:7). In that old story Job held fast to his faith and was finally rewarded by God, while the friends received the heavy censure of God (Job 42:10–17). This old story a later author took and revised, inserting from his own hand the poetical portion that runs from 3:1–42:6. This may seem strange to us but there were no laws of literary copyright in those far-off times and men could do as they pleased with a manuscript. They added or subtracted from it as they thought fit. The great and beautiful poem on Wisdom in chapter 28 is probably a later addition and the speeches of Elihu in chapters 32–37 are regarded by most scholars as added to the original Poem. The Poem itself we may judge to be written with the life-blood of the author who was unable to find satisfaction in the old and current theology. He tells here the story of his own spiritual pilgrimage and how out of all the darkness he attained to a place where all pain was turned to peace and doubts and difficulties vexed no more.

So much we may say about the book and its form. We will now consider what it has to say on the main problem of suffering.

b) THE PROLOGUE TO JOB

The Prologue opens with a view of Job, a man "perfect and upright and one that feared God and turned away from evil." And in exact accord with his piety was his prosperity:

> And there were born unto him seven sons and three daughters. His substance also was seven thousand sheep, and three thousand camels, and five hundred yoke of oxen, and five

hundred she-asses, and a very great household; so that this man was the greatest of all the children of the east.

(Job 1:2, 3)

Here, too, we are ushered into a heavenly council where the "sons of God," that is, His ministering spirits, "present themselves before the Lord, and the Satan came also among them." They are assembled to give an account of their stewardship. Here we see the Satan—we must note the definite article here—who also was one of the Lord's ministering spirits. It will repay us to look more closely at this servant of the Lord.

The word "Satan" means opposer or adversary: it is the word used in Numbers 22:22, 32, where in the story of Balaam and his ass we read

> "The angel of the Lord placed himself in the way for an adversary (literally, for a Satan) against him."

Thus the path of Balaam was blocked and his advance was opposed. Again it is used in I Kings 11:14, 23, 25 thus:

> "The Lord raised up an adversary (Satan) unto Solomon, Hadad the Edomite . . . and God raised up another adversary (Satan) unto him, Rezon, the son of Eliada . . . and he was an adversary (Satan) to Israel all the days of Solomon."

The Psalmist complains that

> "those that render evil for good are adversaries unto me" (literally, Satanize me).   (Psalm 38:20)

And again in Psalm 109:4 we find him saying of the wicked:

> "my love they requite with opposition" (literally, in return for my love they Satanize me).

In the heavenly council the Satan or Adversary is that angel whose function was to oppose men in their pretensions to right-standing before God. Thus in Zechariah 3:1 we see him opposing the claims of Joshua the high priest to occupy his high office. The Satan doubts his fitness. The Satan is concerned for God's glory and his business is to see that no counterfeit piety or camouflaged religion "gets away with it." His function is not unlike that of the *advocatus diaboli* (the Devil's advocate) in the Roman Catholic *curia* whose business it is to challenge and oppose the claims of those presented for canonization. For only so can the saints be proved flawless and blameless. So often in his journeys up and down and through the earth—we can think of him as a district superintendent whose parish was the world!—he has witnessed great shows of piety without any real substance of true religion. So frequent has been this experience that the Satan has become wholly cynical in his estimate of men. Just as the dyer's hand becomes subdued to the element in which it works, the Satan has become used to this kind of thing and he becomes eventually *der Geist der verneint* (the denying spirit). Our word "devil" is derived from the Greek *diabolos*, which means "slanderer." It is not difficult to see how this development took place: one might say it was inevitable.

We can trace the development within the Old Testament. In I Chronicles 21:1 the numbering of the people by David is attributed to the instigation of Satan—now a proper name without the definite article—though in the earlier account found in II Samuel 24:1 the act is ascribed to the prompting of Jehovah himself. By the time of the Chronicler, perhaps about 350 B.C., Satan has become an evil being standing over against and opposing God. But in the Prologue here —and it should be carefully noted—the Satan is one of Jehovah's ministering spirits who does nothing but by the divine permission.

So much it has been necessary to say by way of introduction to this scene in the court of heaven. The Satan comes, as come the others, and in response to the divine query he makes his report.

> And the Lord said unto the Satan, Whence comest thou? Then the Satan answered the Lord, and said, From going to and fro in the earth, and from walking up and down in it. And the Lord said unto the Satan, Hast thou considered my servant Job? for there is none like him in the earth, a perfect and an upright man, one that feareth God and turneth away from evil. Then the Satan answered the Lord, and said, Doth Job fear God for nought? (1:7-9)

There is a note of pride in that phrase, "my servant Job" and we can well understand it. But the Satan is cynical: he has come to doubt the reality of religion anywhere on earth. He does not believe there is such a thing as disinterested religion: men love God not for what He is but for what He gives. All religion is just a system of barter, so much piety for so much prosperity. Religion is a profitable investment and it pays dividends. Here is surely an amazing indictment of the human race! And God accepts the challenge. God is prepared to "bet His life" on Job and to enter into a wager with the Satan.

> And the Lord said unto the Satan, Behold all that he hath is in thy power; only upon himself put not forth thine hand. So the Satan went out from the presence of the Lord. (1:12)

The Satan is permitted to try Job to the uttermost but instead of cursing God and abandoning religion, as the Satan had anticipated and as Job's own wife suggested, Job maintained his piety even when stripped of possessions and family and smitten with grievous disease.

> Then said his wife unto him, Dost thou still hold fast thine integrity? Renounce God and die. But he said unto her,

Thou speakest as one of the foolish women speaketh. What? Shall we receive good at the hand of God, and shall we not receive evil? In all this did not Job sin with his lips. (2:9, 10)

Such briefly is the Prologue and we may be thankful the final editor of the book left us so much. For the Prologue has something to say in reference to our main problem. It tells us that *suffering may have evidential value.* For in all this Job refutes the cynical sneer of the Satan and shows forth the reality of religion.

One or two reflections may be in place here. We note, in the first place, that the discussion is in heaven but the drama is on earth. Job is not in on the discussion in heaven though he is the main party in the drama on earth. "We walk by faith and not by sight." "The secret things belong unto Jehovah our God; but the things that are revealed belong unto us and to our children for ever" (Deuteronomy 29:29 R. V.). That is why heaven for most of us will just be seeing the other side of things, the side of things we could not see here. "What I do thou knowest not now, but thou shalt know hereafter." The sense of tears hangs o'er all mortal things and "now we see through a glass, darkly; but then, face to face" (I Cor. 13:12). The famous French tapestry weavers who wove those magnificent tapestries that we often see in the houses of the great were accustomed to doing all their work from the rear and all that they could see was a mass of loose threads and stitching. But sometimes a man would rise up from his work and pass round to the front to see the glorious design that was being wrought by their patient labor. And the heart of the toiler was satisfied. If we could but see the other side of things! Some day we will understand and with the deep satisfaction of Job we will say, "Now I know."

Again we note something that may be emphasized—and in the Epilogue it is emphasized with a four-fold repetition of the phrase, "my servant Job"—namely, the fact that God's faith in Job is vindicated and the wager is won. We are accustomed to speaking much of our faith in God but it is well that we should see the other side of this—God's faith in us. There is an old legend concerning the Savior that, after he had ascended into glory and taken his seat at the right hand of God, the angel Gabriel approached the Lord of Glory and asked, "What have you done, Lord, for the spread of the Gospel, the propagation of Christian knowledge?" Whereupon Jesus replied, "I have told Peter and John and Mary." Gabriel held up his hands in horror and exclaimed, "Lord, is that all you have done?" "Yes, Gabriel," said Jesus, "that is all, but you don't know my Peter and my John and my Mary." For Jesus knew, as Augustine knew, that "one loving heart sets another heart on fire." God has faith in us and trusts that we will not let him down. God had faith in Job and that faith was vindicated: "my servant Job." Suffering may have evidential value and may prove the reality of disinterested religion. And, as H. W. Robinson remarks, "the blood of the martyrs, and not the ink of its theologies, is the seed of the Church."[7]

[7]H. Wheeler Robinson, *Suffering, Human and Divine* (1940), p. 61.

VII

The Poem of Job

PLAINLY THE AUTHOR of the Poem was not satisfied with the treatment accorded the problem in the old popular tale. The problem still pressed and something more required to be said. And so he wrote this poem with his own heart's blood, for we may take it to be the record of his own experience and the story of how he passed through the dense darkness to come at last to a place that was luminous with God. One cannot but observe that the prose portions are detached and objective, written from the outside, while the Poem is intensely intimate and personal. Here we have the autobiography of one who faced the bleak black hour of the spirit and passed through the thick gloom of night and attained finally the full light of day. And we may be sure that the solution to this problem, if solution there be, will be a solution struck out on the anvil of a broken bleeding heart. It may not be a solution that will satisfy the intellect of man but it may quiet the troubled heart and heal the wounded spirit.

"In the Book of Job," says James Strahan, "nothing less than a campaign of centuries is dramatically compressed into a single decisive battle."[1] And that battlefield is the soul of a suffering man who hews out a new and more satis-

[1]James Strahan, *The Book of Job,* p. 4.

fying creed in the sweat and agony of his bleeding heart. But the conservatism of religion and religious systems is so strong that the introduction of a new idea is likely to be fiercely resisted as a grievous encroachment or looked upon as an act of treason. J. A. Froude remarks wisely in this connection:

> Periods of religious transition, therefore, when the advance has been a real one, always have been violent, and probably will continue to be so. They to whom the precious gift of fresh light has been given are called upon to exhibit their credentials as teachers in suffering for it. They, and those who oppose them, have alike a sacred cause: and the fearful spectacle arises of earnest, vehement men, contending against each other as for their own souls, in fiery struggle. Persecution comes and martyrdoms and religious wars; and at last, the old faith, like the phoenix, expires upon its altar, and the new rises out of the ashes.[2]

All history bears witness to the fact

> That life is not as idle ore,
>
> But iron dug from central gloom,
>   And heated hot with burning fears,
>   And dipt in baths of hissing tears,
> And batter'd with the shocks of doom
>
> To shape and use.[3]

Those who bear witness to new truth must often seal their testimony with their blood: the pioneer must bear the cross.

A word should be said here as to the order of the dialogue in the Poem. Job speaks first (chapter 3), and is followed by Eliphaz (4, 5) to whom Job replies (6, 7). Bildad speaks next (8) followed by another speech from Job (9,

---

[2]John A. Froude, *Short Studies on Great Subjects*, Collins Edn., pp. 236–237.
[3]Alfred Tennyson, *In Memoriam*, CXVIII.

10). Lastly appears Zophar (11) and a speech of Job follows (12–14). For three rounds or cycles this goes on although in the third cycle of speeches there appears to be some dislocation. Bildad seems to say almost nothing while Zophar disappears entirely. Some scholars have assumed that the friends had exhausted their arguments and had nothing more to say.[4] This they take to be part of the poet's art. But this does not seem likely, especially in the case of Zophar who is certainly not the type that could easily be closed out. It seems wiser to assume with most commentators that there has been a certain dislocation of the text at this point and we follow the usual rearrangement of the verses and assign the passages as follows:

25:1, 26:2–4, 25:2–6, 26:5–14	Bildad's third speech.
26:1, 27:2–6, 11–12	Part of Job's reply to Bildad.
27:7, 10, 13–23	Zophar's third speech.

Such a rearrangement of the material makes a natural and clear connection with Job's final speech (29–31). Chapter 28, the Poem on Wisdom, is regarded by most scholars as a later intrusion.

With this preface we may proceed to consider the main subject and, with slight alteration of order, we will follow the plan of H. W. Robinson and consider the problem *a*) from the viewpoint of the friends, *b*) from the side of Job, and *c*) from the standpoint of the Almighty.[5] It may be objected that such a plan does not do justice to the lively flow and interplay of the dialogue and the clash and conflict of the various personalities. Such a method would have a

[4]This view is taken by Artur Weiser in his recent commentary *Das Buch Hiob* (1951).

[5]H. W. Robinson, *The Cross of Job,* London (n. d.: a most valuable little volume, 71 pages).

distinct disadvantage if applied to a Greek tragedy where the interplay of feeling and emotion is too close and integrated to be separated. But in the Poem of Job there is an element of rigidity and almost of the statuesque, for the various speeches seem more like spoken pieces without close relation to each other. Job seems to move forward in his search for inward stability without much reference to the friends or what they say. Nonetheless, there does appear at times a certain sequence in that Job's words are frequently conditioned or suggested by a word or phrase the friends have used. Thus, e.g., his thought of a legal contest (9:1 f.) with the Almighty would seem to stem from Bildad's exposition on the righteousness of God. But normally Job seems lost in contemplation of his own sad case and seems rather to be thinking aloud than directly answering the friends.

a) THE VIEWPOINT OF THE FRIENDS

We may begin here by looking at these three friends. We note that they came to comfort their friend. They did not stay at home and just send a note of condolence. That might have been much easier and less expensive. They left their homes and their business and betook themselves with main haste and resolution to comfort their friend. The measure of their friendship may be gauged by the measure of their sorrow at the sight of their friend.

> And they made an appointment together to come to bemoan and to comfort him. And when they lifted up their eyes afar off, and knew him not, they lifted up their voice and wept; and they rent everyone his mantle, and sprinkled dust upon their heads toward heaven. So they sat down with him upon the ground seven days and seven nights, and none spake a word unto him: for they saw that his grief was very great.
> (2:11–13)

Thus they do honor to his vast grief.

> They do not inflict upon him meaningless commonplaces;
> . . . Eliphaz the Temanite, Bildad the Shuhite, and Zophar
> the Naamathite, sitting in the dust with Job, not daring to
> intrude upon him, are for ever an example of what man
> once was and ought to be to man.[6]

Let this be said at the beginning for those friends of Job,
for they have been much maligned in later times until the
phrase "Job's comforters" has become a byword of rebuke
and vilification.

Eliphaz is the oldest of the three, older than Job, older,
too, than Job's father (15:10). A man of wisdom and piety
he walked in close fellowship with heaven and secret revela-
tions were given him (4:12 f.). He was a man of the inner
light and lovable withal. He handles Job's suffering deli-
cately and with tenderness and seeks to apply the healing
balm. But his patience is not inexhaustible and the flinty
faith of his fathers finally overpowers his friendship for Job.

Bildad is the scholar, wise in the wisdom of the ancients
and skilled in the lore of the past. The traditions of the
fathers must rule among men. The moderns really know
nothing though they have the conceit of knowledge:

> For, inquire, I pray thee, of the former age,
> and apply thyself to that which their fathers have searched
>   out:
> (For we are but of yesterday, and know nothing,
> because our days upon earth are a shadow)
> Shall not they teach thee, and tell thee,
> and utter words out of their hearts?   (8:8–10)

There were giants in those far-off days: Job and his kind are
but pigmies. It may be the antediluvians had more time to

[6]Mark Rutherford (cited by Strahan, *op. cit.*, p. 48).

gather wisdom, but the record does not bear out the contention of Bildad.

Zophar is the least distinct and most general of the friends; he may represent the man in the street: he is rough and ready, very rough and very ready. His tongue when it gets to wagging is sharper than a two-edged sword. If Bildad is the Traditionalist then Zophar is the Dogmatist, and his dogmatism is in inverse proportion to any real knowledge.

Such are the friends of Job who came to comfort him and remained to abuse him: their harsh and flinty theology was more to them than their friend. Face to face with a new and unprecedented situation they deal with it in the good old-fashioned way!

Eliphaz speaks first and with gentle probing he seeks to uncover the wound. He emphasizes the transcendent purity of God before whom no unclean thing can stand. Suffering may be God's call to a man to examine himself. It may be the divine discipline.

> Behold, happy is the man whom God correcteth;
> therefore despise not thou the chastening of the Almighty.
> For he maketh sore, and bindeth up:
> he woundeth, and his hands make whole.   (5:17, 18)

Here Eliphaz unconsciously sets a thought in Job's mind, a thought that was not there before—God is the author of Job's suffering. We shall see what Job made of this. But Eliphaz is too old to recognize a new problem—the problem of suffering innocence. This new thing cannot be classified with any ancient formula or fitted into the accepted scheme of things. Eliphaz has no key in all his girdle to open this door nor will his visions of the night avail to unlock this mystery. "Job and the world need a new book of comfort and Eliphaz is scarcely the person to write it" (Strahan).

Bildad takes up the parable from a slightly different angle. He stresses the divine righteousness—and here he, too, puts a thought in Job's mind which Job will push to its issue— and in so doing he will out-Calvin Calvin. There is a failure on the part of the friends to disentangle the thought of the divine righteousness from the divine wisdom and power. Righteousness here is something arbitrary on which man cannot rely: right and wrong are just what the Almighty decrees them to be. It is this question of the divine righteousness that stirs Job to some of his wildest words as we shall see presently.

Zophar, as we have said, is the sharpest-tongued of the friends, as he is also the shallowest. His opinions are second-hand but he holds them strongly and expresses them with extreme dogmatism. Here we have the voice of popular wisdom. It is perhaps understandable that a sense of irritation and exasperation should be produced in the friends by Job's recalcitrant attitude and his wild whirling words. They could not be expected to approve of his cavalier dismissal of all their arguments. After all, they were men of distinction and of high standing; they represented public opinion. Thus we can understand Zophar's blunt words: Job is but a windbag and is just doing harm to religion.

> Then answered Zophar the Naamathite, and said,
> Should not the multitude of words be answered?
> and should a man full of talk (literally, a man of lips) be
>   justified?
> Should men be silent at thy babblings?
>
> .   .   .   .   .   .
>
> Know therefore that God exacteth of thee less than thine
>   iniquity deserveth.   (11:1–3, 6)

In the second cycle of speeches the friends concentrate

on a series of lurid pictures of the fate of the wicked with
a finger constantly pointed at Job as if to say, "Thou art the
man." There is an increasing sense of exasperation and even
the gentle Eliphaz does not hesitate to suggest that Job is
nothing but a windbag:

> Should a wise man make answer with vain knowledge,
> and fill his belly with the east wind?
> Should he reason with unprofitable talk,
> or with speeches wherewith he can do no good?   (15:2, 3)

Bildad repudiates the rage and scorn of Job for his friends:

> Wherefore are we counted as beasts,
> have we become dumb in your sight?   (18:3)

and he closes his speech against Job with the vicious punch-
line:

> Surely such are the dwellings of the unrighteous,
> and this is the place of him that knoweth not God.   (18:21)

This same pattern is followed by Zophar in 20:29: there is
no mistaking the direction of his remarks:

> This is the portion of a wicked man from God,
> and the heritage appointed unto him by God.

The white radiance of eternity is apt to be stained more
than a little when it is transmitted by such hands and hearts.

In the third cycle of speeches Eliphaz comes out with a
definite series of specific charges against Job:

> Is not thy wickedness great?
> neither is there any end to thine iniquities.
> For thou hast taken pledges of thy brother for nought,
> and stripped the naked of their clothing.
> Thou hast not given water to the weary to drink,
> and thou hast withholden bread from the hungry . . .
> Thou hast sent widows away empty,
> and the arms of the fatherless have been broken.
>   (22:5-7, 9)

How could Eliphaz avoid coming to this conclusion? "All sufferers are sinners," therefore, "Great sufferers are great sinners." The *rabies dogmatica* must run its course and this is its final issue. Job is "the chief of sinners." *Tantum religio potuit suadere malorum.*[7] What crimes have been wrought in the name of religion! Their hearts were chilled by a frozen creed and their friend was sacrificed on the altar of an effete theology.

In the third cycle the poet reveals his art by making Bildad repeat the theme of the first cycle, the incomparable greatness of God, while Zophar repeats the theme of the second cycle, the miserable fate of the wicked. In this last speech of Zophar the Dogmatist concludes with a terrifying picture of the laughing and jeering God:

> For God shall hurl at him, and not spare:
> he would fain flee out of his hand.
> Men shall clap their hands at him,
> and shall hiss him out of his place.   (27:22, 23)

Sinners in the hands of an angry God! The God of Zophar does everything that Zophar would do if he were in God's place.

> "That He should clap His hands in anger over an impenitent sinner, and hiss at him in scorn, is all quite natural. How often the poet had heard just such sentiments expressed in just such language! It is his purpose to hold up all this bad theology and crude anthropomorphism to eternal reprobation."[8]

b) THE ATTITUDE OF JOB

In the Prologue we observe Job's attitude of profound resignation. In adversity as in prosperity Job sinned not with

---

[7]Lucretius, *De Rerum Natura,* I:102
[8]J. Strahan, *op. cit.,* p. 230.

his lips. "The Lord gave and the Lord hath taken away: blessed be the name of the Lord." The piety of Job and his genuine religion were fully vindicated and approved.

But with the opening words of chapter 3 we enter another atmosphere and we hear an exceeding bitter cry. Job opens his lips and he curses his day:

> Let the day perish wherein I was born,
> and the night which said, There is a man conceived.
> Let that day be darkness;
> let not God regard it from above,
> neither let the light shine upon it.
> Let darkness and the shadow of death claim it for
> their own.   (3:3–5)

Here the poet reveals psychological insight for he knows that the faith that was strong to withstand the first assaults of outrageous fortune, great and overwhelming, may faint and fail under the growing pressure of continued suffering. It takes Job some time—we may presume the lapse of some weeks—to realize what has come upon him and the utter hopelessness of his lot. Job breaks down and Job breaks out in this way, for life is now nothing but a living death. Better far to be dead and gone than to drag out wearisome nights and interminable days in never-ending and irremediable pain:

> Wherefore is light given to him that is in misery,
> and life unto the bitter in soul;
> Which long for death, but it cometh not;
> and dig for it more than for hid treasures;
> Which rejoice exceedingly
> and are glad, when they can find the grave?
> *Why is light given* to a man whose way is hid,
> and whom God hath hedged in?   (3:20–23)

This is a natural cry, like the cry of a wounded animal, and

Job would be less than human if he did not express himself in this fashion. Strangely enough throughout the Poem Job does not seek death but rather life, and it should be noted that the thought of suicide never enters his mind.

It is to be observed that both Job and the friends hold the same philosophy of life. Their theology was his theology though none of them had ever thought that theology through to its ultimate issues. But Job is now forced to think it through: the friends employ the method of the mosquito and by their insistent attack they goad Job onwards and upwards until he finally attains inward stability. As we have remarked already Job does not seem to deal directly with the friends and their harsh imputations: their irritation and growing sense of exasperation are largely due to the fact that they are overlooked by Job, for Job is occupied with larger matters than the opinions of men. Throughout the dialogue Job is fearfully dynamic while the friends are wholly static: their God is a tradition, their religion a conventionalism. They are zealous for the forms and decorum of religion, but they express no longing for direct spiritual communion with the living God. But two certainties remain throughout in the mind of Job and he never lets them go. In the first place he has tasted the goodness of God and he cannot deny the reality of that communion and fellowship with the divine. In the second place he is conscious of his own integrity and he will not set the lie in his own soul by denying a mind conscious of its rectitude, an extreme rectitude that has been attested by Yahwe Himself though Job is unaware of that fact. These two certainties never fade from the mind of Job and it is precisely because of their presence that the tragic schism is set within the soul of Job. His loneliness here is the loneliness of the depth and it is deeper and more profound than the loneliness of Jeremiah, for while Jeremiah was alone with God against the world Job is in the more tragic position of being alone against God and the world. For only thus can he assert finally the moral rights of personality and maintain the dignity of man. Job is pre-eminently a Protestant and he would have understood well the words of John Stuart Mill:

> I will call no being good who is not what I mean when I apply that epithet to my fellow-creature; and if such a being will sentence me to hell for not calling him so to hell I will go.[9]

That is the question: is God "such a being"? Job cannot forget "the blessedness that once I knew" and he will not believe that the divine friend has now changed into a fiend with hostile intent. The ministry of memory keeps plying his heart with subtle tenderness and he knows there is no flight from God but unto God.

> Oh that thou wouldest hide me in Sheol,
> that thou wouldest keep me secret, until thy wrath be past,
> that thou wouldest appoint me a set time, and remember me!
> If a man die shall he live *again?*
> all the days of my warfare would I wait,
> till my release should come.
> Thou shouldest call and I would answer thee;
> thou wouldest have a desire unto the work of thy hands.
>
> (14:13–15)

Job cannot forget—and Job does not believe God can forget—the sweet communion and fellowship that once were his:

> Oh that I were as in the months of old,
> as in the days when God watched over me;

[9] J. S. Mill, *An Examination of Sir William Hamilton's Philosophy* (1884), p. 131.

When his lamp shined upon my head,
and by his light I walked through darkness.   (29:2, 3)

It is this that sets Job at odds with himself. The theology
he had inherited leads him to say that God is unjust and
immoral while his experience, which he may not deny, at-
tests God's goodness:

> The God of the past and the future was the real God. Job's
> God of the present was the spectre of the morbid imagina-
> tion.[10]

This tragic schism first comes to light in the mind of Job
after the speech of Eliphaz. Yahwe is the author of Job's suffering. "Surely an enemy hath done this." Yahwe who was his
friend has become his foe. Yahwe is unjust. For Job knows
he has committed no sin to merit such vast suffering. Bildad
may hymn the transcendent greatness of God and Zophar
expatiate on the inscrutability of the divine wisdom but Job
suffers as an innocent man. Where is the divine righteousness? God is great and we need no Bildad to tell us that,
but "his ways are not equal."

> It is all one; therefore I say,
> He destroyeth the perfect and the wicked.
> If the scourge slay suddenly,
> he will mock at the trial of the innocent.
> The earth is given into the hand of the wicked;
> he covereth the faces of the judges thereof;
> if *it be* not *he*, who then is it?   (9:22–24)

At this point in the dialogue there comes to the mind of
Job the thought of a contest-at-law. Bildad had harped at
length on the thought of the divine righteousness (*tsedeq*)
and it is this that stirs the thought in Job's mind:

[10]A. S. Peake, "Job" (*Century Bible*), p. 16.

> Doth God pervert judgment (*mishpat*)
> and doth Shaddai pervert justice (*tsedeq*)?   (8:3)

Perish the thought, says Bildad. The Judge of all the earth shall do right: His judgments are just. Now this word *tsedeq* and its derivatives are originally terms associated with a law court; their meaning is forensic. *Tsaddiq* (righteous) is the term applied to one who wins a lawsuit while *Rasha'* (wicked) is the term applied to the loser. The terms originally have nothing to do with character for in an Oriental court the *Tsaddiq* might be cast in the suit (*Rasha'*) and the *Rasha'* might be hailed by the judge as *Tsaddiq*. But there was enough moral insight in old Israel to discern that this was not as it should be, and those who "justify the wicked for reward" (Isaiah 5:23) are continually denounced. Thus by an easily understood development the term *Tsaddiq* came to have ethical content and acquired the meaning of one who ought to win his suit. Thus throughout the Psalter we find the Righteous (*Tsaddiqim*) standing together with the Saints (*Chasidim*) over against the Wicked (*Rĕsha'im*) and the Sinners (*Chattaim*). Thus the term received distinct ethical quality. At times it may not be easy to discern the exact shade of meaning—both meanings may be present in the speech of Bildad—but Job fastens on the legal angle. He thinks of a contest-at-law. But who can hope to contend with Shaddai (the Almighty)? Frail mortal man has no chance to prove his innocence before omnipotence:

> Of a truth I know that it is so;
> but how can a man be just with God?
> If he be pleased to contend with him,
> he cannot answer him one of a thousand . . .
> How much less shall I answer him,
> and choose out my words *to reason* with him?   (9:2, 3, 14)

How could Job maintain his cause before the Almighty who can change right into wrong? Is a thing right because Shaddai declares it so, or does he declare it right because it is so? That is Job's problem: *the character of God is at stake:*

> The book aims not at solving the entire problem of suffering but at vindicating God and the latent worth of human nature against certain conclusions drawn from a partial observation of life.[11]

But if man may not be permitted to contend directly with God might it not yet be possible to reason together?

> For he is not man, as I am, that I should answer him,
> that we should come together in judgment.
> There is no daysman betwixt us,
> that might lay his hand upon us both.   (9:32, 33)

This thought of an arbitrator or mediator leads Job to a new and daring approach and in this approach we see the tragic schism carried a point further, even into the heart of God Himself. Clearly there is no help in man and there is no refuge from God save in God Himself. The high God must be invoked against the low God, the God of things as they ought to be against the God of things as they are, the God of Job's experience against the God of Job's theology.[12] If God be against him who can be for him but God? The God for whom his tears flow must aid him against the God who is his antagonist. There is something amazing in the juxtaposition of these phrases and ideas:

> My friends scorn me:
> *but* mine eye poureth out tears unto God;

[11]S. R. Driver and G. B. Gray, *International Critical Commentary; Job,* p. LI. Cp. Weiser, *op. cit.,* p 13
[12]Artur Weiser, *op. cit.,* p. 17.

that he would maintain the right of a man with God,
and of a son of man with his neighbor!   (16:20, 21)

The last line may seem particularly daring and many commentators water it down, but what it seems to say is that the
neighbor of Job, frail mortal man (son of man), is God. In
any case the logical incoherence of this passage cannot hide
from us its religious depth. The distinction Job seeks to draw
is a distinction between seemingly contradictory moods in
the being of God Himself. To this logical contradiction Job
is brought through the clash of experience—interpreted in
terms of an effete theology—with his moral sense through
which, all unconsciously, he is in process of shaping a more
adequate theology. Job will not rest until he stands again in
the presence of God, for in his heart he knows that God is
good.

At this point one must raise the question of how far his
thought of the hereafter enters into the mind of Job. We
know that when this thought does emerge in the Old Testament it emerges in close connection with the thought of
innocent suffering. This we see clearly in the Psalter.[13] It
may be that the poet intended to represent Job as a brave
soul who fights his battle and "drees his weird"[14] solely
within the bounds of space and time and that he had no
thought of life hereafter. But the record does not sustain this
position and no one can read the poem without being sensi-
ble of the fact that Job does harbor thoughts of life hereafter. Such a thought lies behind his repeated plaints concerning the brevity of life:

Now my days are swifter than a post:
they flee away, they see no good.   (9:25)

[13]See the author's *Praises of Israel* (1950), pp. 230–245.
[14]*Scotticé:* "fulfills his allotted destiny."

My days are swifter than a weaver's shuttle,
and are spent without hope.
O, remember that my life is wind:
mine eye shall see no good.
The eye of him that seeth me shall behold me no more:
thine eye shall be upon me, but I shall not be.   (7:6-8)

The Hebrew loved life and length of days but only life as it was lived in the favor of God was worthy of the name. It was inevitable that out of such faith should grow the assurance of life hereafter and that what was implicit in the Hebrew faith should become explicit:

> Thine are these orbs of light and shade;
>   Thou madest Life in man and brute;
>   Thou madest Death; and lo, thy foot
> Is on the skull which thou hast made.
>
> Thou wilt not leave us in the dust:
>   Thou madest man, he knows not why,
>   He thinks he was not made to die;
> And thou hast made him: thou art just.[15]

We feel throughout the poem a certain resentment against the indignity of death and the thought of life hereafter rises as a moral postulate even as Job mentions such a hope only to set it aside:

> There is hope of a tree, if it be cut down, that it will sprout
>   again,
> and that the tender branch thereof will not cease.
> Though the root thereof wax old in the earth,
> and the stock thereof die in the ground;
> Yet through the scent of water it will bud,
> and forth boughs like a plant.
> But man dieth, and wasteth away:
> yea, man giveth up the ghost, and where is he?   (14:7-10)

or again in 14:14;

[15]Alfred Tennyson, *In Memoriam* (Prologue).

If a man die, shall he live *again*?

It matters not how we translate this last verse; it may be rendered: "O that one might live again," but the thought is essentially the same. It may be that arguments for immortality drawn from analogies in the natural realm may not bear all the weight their advocates set upon them but Job will not deny the natural instincts of the believing heart. The very repudiation of these suggestions confirms their strength and reality.

Thus we come to the great passage in 19:25 f. and though the text of the passage is very corrupt and countless emendations have been made on it, the present writer feels that the thought of life hereafter or immortality is here expressed:

> But I know that my Redeemer liveth,
> and that he shall stand up at the last upon the earth:
> And after my skin hath been thus destroyed,
> yet from my flesh shall I see God:
> Whom I shall see for myself,
> and mine eyes shall behold, and not another.
> my reins are consumed within me.

The word translated "redeemer" is the Hebrew word *Go'el,* which means vindicator, the next of kin, whose solemn duty it was to do right by the dead, either in the way of avenging his death or carrying out the proper property dispositions as required by law, in general, "to show loyalty (*Chesed*) to the dead." It is the word frequently used by Second Isaiah to denote the redeemer of Israel.

Now it seems psychologically imperative at this point in the debate that some such word should come here. The debate between Job and the friends has mounted to such a point of intensity that some relief is required in the tense emotional situation. If such relief does not come something will snap and break: Job may lose the kindly light of reason unless here there be interposed some *Deus ex machina* to loosen the knot. There comes in all high tragedy precisely such a point where tension must be relieved. The emotions of the auditors become too taut and tense and some relief of the strain must be given. Thus one might wonder why Shakespeare set the ribald and ridiculous Porter scene in *Macbeth* but Shakespeare was skilled in the dramatist's art and knew what he was doing. The sense of revulsion and moral horror produced by the murder of the gracious King Duncan imposed a strain on the emotions of the auditors and that strain had to be relieved: Shakespeare does that with the Porter scene. And the dramatist here—if we may call him dramatist—was no less skilled. For a moment he allows the veil to be rent and Job sees to the other side: the deepest instincts of his heart are confirmed and he faints for very joy and exultation. God is not a Fiend, as his theology led him to say: God is a Friend, as his heart always knew.

T. H. Robinson compares this passage with Psalm 73:23 f. and certainly in the Psalter passage the experience involved is almost identical with that in Job. With reference to the life hereafter Robinson says in reference to Job 19:25 f.:

> Here at last is envisaged a life after death in which he will still remain in touch with God.[16]

Robinson goes further than the present writer would feel justified in going and holds that here we have something like the Greek conception of an immortal spirit. But the normal thought of the Hebrew was the thought of resurrection: the Hebrew could not easily conceive of a spirit without a body. Paul, too, is Hebrew in his thought of resurrection (I Cor. 15). The Greek thought of the matter in an-

[16]T. H. Robinson, *Poetry and Poets of the Old Testament* (1947), p. 99.

other way, for to him the soul was imprisoned in "this muddy vesture of decay," and must be finally freed from the body. To the Greek, man was an incarnate soul, but to the Hebrew he was an animated personality, a *nefesh chayya.* "The poet," says Robinson, was

> a pioneer and had broken loose from all established tradition. It is less surprising, then, that he should have conceived of the future life in a form in which it could hardly find general acceptance among his direct successors. But he did reach this point, and out of the bitterness of his soul and the horror of his experience, he formed a belief which has changed the whole outlook of the human spirit.[17]

This may seem to attribute too much to Job's questing spirit and creative insight. For such a doctrine is first found in Greece towards the end of the fifth century B.C. and a similar idea may be found in *The Wisdom of Solomon,* which cannot be dated earlier than the first century B.C. and may really belong to the early first century A.D. It seems difficult to assume the presence of such an idea in Job. The idea of immortality or life hereafter arose in Greece through logic and psychology, but to the Hebrew it came through his theology and ethic. The Greek began with man as the object of his study but the Hebrew interest was centered in God.

Some commentators (e.g. Peake, T. H. Robinson) think the book at this point comes to a natural division. By this vision Job's personal problem is solved and the later discussion in the following chapters deals with the more general question of divine Providence. This should not be accentuated: there can be no clean cut between these two problems because Job's personal problem is part of the larger problem. Job's vision of his future vindication could not but make a certain difference to him and we may sense a degree of re-

---

[17]T. H. Robinson, *ibid.*

laxation and perhaps serenity in the following speeches of
Job. We may sense also a growing degree of exasperation
on the part of the friends in the increased fury of their assaults. This may be due to Job's changed attitude which
seems to infuriate the friends.

Perhaps, however, we should seek another explanation of
the continuing debate. It would seem that in all such experiences recorded in the Old Testament those concerned had
difficulty in interpreting completely the meaning of their
experience. For such experience was a thing new and unprecedented and could not be easily set into the normal
framework of things. They were "the first to burst into the
unknown sea" and they could not interpret fully what they
saw and heard. Thus Jeremiah speaks his great word on the
New Covenant but he did not comprehend what a large
word he had spoken: that word had to await its full explica-
tion by the Lord of Glory on that night in which he was
betrayed: "This is the new covenant in my blood." Nor could
the singer in Psalm 73 know the full content of the massive
word he uttered, a word on which men later built their assurance of immortality. So here for a moment Job saw the sur-
passing light that was to be eclipsed and obscured by the
subsequent debate. Men must return from the heights to the
valleys where the mists and fogs obscure the vision. So Job
returns to his wrangling and the vision is mainly lost in the
light of common days and mean and petty things. But Eliphaz, Bildad, and Zophar cannot remove the radiant certainty that has filled his mind and he presses on in his quest.
That was but the earnest of his inheritance. The sense of his
own moral integrity and his fundamental assurance of God
as friend will bring him at last where he desires to be. The
world is here looking on a faith that rises above all that is

prudential and calculating by the sheer love of truth. Here we see a man holding to his chosen path by his grip upon reality, acquiring strength and moral capacity because he is pure from all self-seeking aims. "His strength is as the strength of ten, because his heart is pure," and, "The pure in heart shall see God."

An interesting parallel to this may be found in the life of F. W. Robertson who in many ways resembles Job for he, too, was acquainted with sickness that darkened his spirit. He, too, knew the loneliness of the depth. He writes thus:

> It is an awful moment when the soul begins to find that the props on which it has blindly rested so long are, many of them, rotten, and begins to suspect them all; when it begins to feel the nothingness of many of the traditionary opinions which have been received with implicit confidence. . . . In that fearful loneliness of spirit when those who should have been friends and counsellors only frown upon his misgivings and profanely bid him stifle doubts which, for aught he knows, may arise from the fountain of truth itself; to extinguish, as a glare from hell, that which, for aught he knows, may be the light of heaven. . . . I know but one way in which a man may come forth from his agony scathless; it is by holding fast to those things which are certain still—the grand, simple landmarks of morality. If there be no God and no future state, yet even then it is better to be generous than selfish, better to be chaste than licentious, better to be true than false, better to be brave than to be a coward. Blessed beyond all earthly blessedness is the man who, in the tempestuous darkness of the soul, has dared to hold fast to those venerable landmarks. Thrice blessed is he who— when all is drear and cheerless within and without, when his teachers terrify him and his friends shrink from him—has obstinately clung to moral good. Thrice blessed, because *his* night shall pass into clear, bright day.[18]

[18]Stopford A. Brooke, *Life, Letters, Lectures and Addresses of F. W. Robertson* (1871), p. 86.

Blood, sweat and tears are the portion of those who seek the truth and the final vision is won in the sweat of man's heart.

We can set aside all that the friends say in the third cycle of speeches for such things should not be said. But Job's sole concern is to see God more clearly and in the great oath of purgation (chapter 31) where we have the highest statement of Old Testament ethics we see him standing like a prince among men. God surely loves an honest thinker and to the seeking searching spirit light will not be denied.

c) THE DIVINE RESPONSE

Considerable difficulty has been felt by many in regard to the divine speech or speeches. In the first place the text is not easy to read and most scholars are of opinion that we have considerable additions here. The labored descriptions of the hippopotamus and the crocodile (40:15–41:34)[19] seem to interrupt the natural and obvious connection between 40:1–14 and 42:1: they are probably later additions and were not in the original poem.

Again many have found difficulty with the divine speech because it fails to answer the main problem. Budde speaks of the speech as "a piece of devilish irony" and prefers to seek a solution in the contribution of Elihu.[20] But the great majority of scholars regard the Elihu speeches as a later addition and any reader may observe how naturally the words of 31:35 f. set the stage for the introduction of the Deity.

The book deals with the problem of suffering and it seems natural to think that if any light is shed on that question it will be found in the speech of the Almighty. But no direct answer to the problem is offered here. What we have is a

[19]The Hebrew chapter divisions are different: Ch. 41:1 corresponds to 41:9 of the English version.

[20]K. Budde, *Einleitung in das Alte Testament,* (Second Edition), p. 232.

magnificent description of the wonders of Nature that seem worlds away from the problem which vexes Job. And yet that may be the answer and from Job's adoring response, "I had heard of thee by the hearing of the ear; but now mine eye seeth thee" (42:5) we must judge that there is something significant in the speech from the whirlwind. Job clearly indicates that through the display of the divine power and the vastness of the sphere in which God operates he has received a new view of things. Knowledge that was formerly secondhand has now become direct and immediate. What he had heard from others as tradition gives place to first-hand knowledge. "Now I know."

We may look more closely at this. In the first place, we see that Job is taken out of himself and set in the framework of the universe. And so is Job's suffering. It is set in the context of the macrocosm. It has been said that the world of a sick man begins at his pillow and ends at the foot of his bed, and there is a large degree of truth in that word. Suffering tends to shut us in physically and mentally. Our main thought, when we are sick, is to get well and to be released from this cramping, confining thing. We become centered in ourselves and our malady, the microcosm of self. It is something to lift a man out of self and his self-centered world and give him a wider prospect and a broader view. The world is bigger than he dreamed, bigger than the area between his pillow and the foot of his bed, and the spirit of man needs to be "stabbed broad awake" to the realization of that fact. The world seems to be run by intelligence: there is purpose in it and behind that purpose is a Person. Suffering may be part of His purpose.

Again here is revealed the might and wisdom of God. The singer in Psalm 104 saw that clearly and Job sees it here.

But is there love in it? That is the question and the divine speech surely answers that question. For Job sees that God

> causes it to rain on a land where no man is;
> on the wilderness, wherein there is no man;
> To satisfy the waste and desolate *ground;*
> and to cause the tender grass to spring forth.   (38:26, 27)

O foolish and slow to believe! "If God so clothe the grass of the field, which to-day is, and to-morrow is cast into the oven, shall he not much more clothe you, O ye of little faith?" (Matthew 6:30). That thought had not entered the minds of Eliphaz, Bildad, and Zophar but it was clearly revealed to Job, and Job was satisfied. The intuitions of his heart and the promptings of his moral sense were confirmed:

> From the first, Power was—I knew:
> Life has made clear to me,
> That, strive but for a clearer view,
> Love were as plain to see.[21]

We have a great God and we have a good God. God is love. From the dark world of life's uncertainties Job is led into a cosmos that is radiant with God. He is lifted "into the heavenlies" where those vexing questions vex no more and all pain is turned to peace. "The heart has reasons that the reason does not know" (Pascal). Job gets no answer to satisfy the intellect, but he gets a vision that swallows up every problem and fills his heart with a peace the world cannot give and cannot take away. He is consumed and quickened by the vision of God.

> Sorrow is hard to bear, and doubt is slow to clear,
> Each sufferer says his say, his scheme of the weal and woe:
> But God has a few of us whom he whispers in the ear;
> The rest may reason and welcome: 't is we musicians know.[22]

[21]R. Browning, *Asolando.*   [22]R. Browning, *Abt Vogler.*

"The secret of the Lord is with them that fear him" (Psalm 25:14) or better with the Revised Version, "The friendship of Jehovah is with them that fear him." Having God as friend, what needs a man more?

What more does Job need? Nothing. But the old story must have a happy ending, and the Epilogue supplies it. But Job needs no piece of silver or earrings of gold or those seven sons and three daughters with the high-sounding names. Job has God and having Him, he has more than all. We know that well but the old story had to make it clear to common folk and this is how he did it. It was not anti-climax to him; it was consummation and fulfillment.

The present writer has often wondered at the marvelous insight of this old story-teller. As he tells of the restoration of Job's property he relates how everything was doubled— everything except his family. Did not the writer show strange spiritual insight here? Did he not say something bigger and better than he knew? Were not he and William Words-worth spiritually one?

> "Sisters and brothers, little maid,
> How many may you be?"
> "How many? Seven in all," she said,
> And wondering looked at me.

> "And where are they? I pray you tell."
> She answered, "Seven are we:
> And two of us at Conway dwell,
> And two are gone to sea.

> "Two of us in the church-yard lie,
> My sister and my brother;
> And in the church-yard cottage, I
> Dwell near them with my mother."

> "You say that two at Conway dwell,

And two are gone to sea,
Yet ye are seven! I pray you tell,
Sweet maid, how this may be."

Then did the little maid reply,
"Seven boys and girls are we;
Two of us in the church-yard lie,
Beneath the church-yard tree."

"You run about, my little Maid,
Your limbs they are alive;
If two are in the church-yard laid,
Then ye are only five."

.   .   .   .   .

"How many are you, then," said I,
"If they two are in heaven?"
Quick was the little Maid's reply,
"O Master! we are seven."

"But they are dead; those two are dead!
Their spirits are in heaven!"
'Twas throwing words away; for still
The little maid would have her will,
And said, "Nay, we are seven!"

"Out of the mouths of babes and sucklings hast thou ordained strength." Job had seven sons and three daughters here and seven sons and daughters there. The Greek translators must have shared this insight when they added to the last words of the Epilogue—"So Job died, being old and full of days"—these additional words:

And it is written that he will rise again with those whom the Lord raises up.

VIII

Ecclesiastes

THE BOOK OF ECCLESIASTES is not as well known as it should be, though Renan called it the most lovable book written by a Jew. On a first reading its contents may appear rather startling and bewildering. Scholars seem puzzled by it. To Heine it was *the Hymn of Scepticism,* while to the great commentator Franz Delitzsch it was *the Hymn of Godly Fear.* To another (Ludwig Levy) it records the story of a shipwrecked faith, while Hertzberg sees in it "one of the most startling Messianic prophecies of the Old Testament."[1] To Morris Jastrow, Ecclesiastes is "a Gentle Cynic,"[2] while Johannes Pedersen discusses the book under the title "*Israelite Scepticism.*"[3] Such variety of opinion among competent scholars may seem as bewildering as Ecclesiastes himself, but it shows at least that the book is of great human interest.

a) THE AUTHOR AND HIS DATE

How Ecclesiastes came to be in the Bible is a story no less interesting. It had great difficulty in making the grade and was only received into the Old Testament Canon after long and heated debate. Those assembled at Jamnia about 100

[1]L. W. Hertzberg, *Der Prediger* (Qohelet) (1932), p. 47.
[2]Morris Jastrow, *A Gentle Cynic* (1919).
[3]Johannes Pedersen, *Scepticisme Israélite* (1931).

A.D., the group of scholars to whom was committed the responsibility of deciding which books should be regarded as Holy Scripture, had no difficulty in deciding about most of the books but as to the merits of three particular writings they were uncertain. Those three were, as we have seen, Ecclesiastes, the Song of Songs, and the book of Esther. Our primary concern here is with Ecclesiastes. "Does Ecclesiastes defile the hands?" was the question asked, that is, must one approach it with ritual precautions required in the handling of sacred books? Is it sacred or secular? The school of Shammai opposed the acceptance of Ecclesiastes but the school of Hillel stood for it and Hillel prevailed. But even when the verdict was given and Ecclesiastes admitted to the Canon many continued to look askance at it and questioned the wisdom of what had been done. It is well to have this in mind as we judge the book: if those Jews of that early period had such doubts and misgivings as to its merits, there may have been some good reasons for their hesitation.

There was a reason. Ecclesiastes represents the mood of scepticism and thoroughgoing scepticism at that, as we shall soon see. Though scepticism has been common enough throughout the ages we hardly expect to find it in a book that purportedly sets forth the fundamental truth of things. Yet it would have been a great pity and a serious loss if a book that is meant to be the Bible of all men made no reference or failed to deal with the mood of scepticism which is common to all men. We may not doubt that in this matter the council was rightly guided when it decided to admit Qoheleth[4] and we are thankful that the book is there.

Regarding the name Qoheleth which we have just used, this is a Hebrew word derived from a root meaning "to as-

[4]Frequently written as *Koheleth*.

semble." Peculiarly enough the form is feminine though it is clearly a male who speaks. This form is to be explained by the fact that in Semitic usage, particularly in Arabic, such forms are frequently used to designate the official who holds the office. Such terms referred originally to the office or function and clearly something of this kind is here implied. The Greek version translated Qoheleth by *Ecclesiastes*, which signifies a member of the assembly (*ecclesia*) and the Latin made it *concionator*, which means one who calls an assembly or meeting. Luther translated it with the word *Prediger*, which means preacher, and in most modern languages he is called the Preacher. This old sage would surely have laughed loud and long if he had thought that one day men would array him in the preacher's gown! So we may call him Qoheleth or Ecclesiastes or the Preacher as we will. As to his being a king of any kind most scholars set that aside as a literary addition or a mere literary pose—common enough in Egypt—and Qoheleth does not maintain that role beyond the second chapter: in the last chapter (12:8) he is referred to simply as a sage (*chakam*). Monarchs retired from business have frequently set forth their reflections on life but there is no reason to think we have such here.

As to the date of the book we shall not be wide of the mark if we date it about 250–225 B.C. Some scholars would date it later and a date as late as that of Herod the Great (39–4 B.C.) has been suggested. A date in the Greek period when the Ptolemies were in the ascendant seems most probable.

The language of the book points to such a period: the language is certainly later than Ezra, Nehemiah, and Malachi. No other book of the Old Testament shows such a relatively strong Aramaic flavor and some of the Preacher's words and phrases seem to be Greek words in Hebrew form. The ideas expressed in the book would have found no place in the Maccabean period but they agree well with the date suggested. Some scholars have thought the book was first written in Aramaic and translated into Hebrew, but there is no sound ground for this assumption.

As to where it was written, scholars have contended for Egypt and Palestine. Those who think of Egypt as its place of origin refer to such passages as speak of great rivers and harbors (1:7; 11:1) but there is nothing in these passages which an ordinary educated layman might not know. Ecclesiastes had, in all probability, traveled widely and he knew geography. There seems no good reason to look beyond Jerusalem for the point of origin of the book and such references as 5:1; 11:4; 12:2 seem to point that way.

Regarding the structure of the book, opinions vary. Some find here almost as many strands as occur in the Pentateuch and critical analysis has been pushed to extremes. Thus Siegfried[5] finds nine different hands at work in the book while McNeile[6] is satisfied with three. But the strange thing about this book is that it displays a more uniform style than any other book of the Old Testament and in recent times stress has rightly been laid upon the unity of the writing. Apart from minor additions (2:26; 3:17; 7:26b; 8:5; 8:12b, 13a; 11:9a; 12:7b), it seems wiser to treat the work as that of a single author. Most commentators agree that the original work ended at 12:8 and that 12:9–11 and 12:12–14 represent two epilogues probably added by students of the sage.

b) METHOD AND PROCEDURE

A word should be said here as to the method and pro-

---

[5]D. C. Siegfried, *Prediger und Hoheslied* (1898).
[6]A. H. McNeile, *An Introduction to Ecclesiastes* (1904).

cedure of the Preacher. He is a profound empiricist. He examines life, but there is no logical order in his examination: he just seems to be thinking aloud. His method is usually to begin with a common saying or current proverb which he introduces with the words "I saw" or "I observed." He then proceeds to turn the saying around as he looks closely at it from all sides and finally his own view is introduced with the words, "I knew" or "I said to myself."

> Then I saw that wisdom excelleth folly, as far as light excelleth darkness. The wise *man's* eyes are in his head; but the fool walketh in darkness. . . . Then said I in my heart, As it happeneth to the fool so it happeneth to me, even me; and why was I then more wise? Then said I in my heart, that this also is vanity.   (2:13–15)

Or, again, he may state his belief and proceed to confirm it by instances and examples adduced: thus all that follows 1:2 confirms his opening word. Or yet again he will quote a proverb or current saying for his jumping-off point (7:1; 10:2) or he may set the proverb at the end of his section (1:15; 4:12; 7:7; 8:1). The book falls easily into sections. Hertzberg divides it into twelve such sections and allows for subdivisions.[7] Budde finds twenty-three main sections and also allows for subdivisions,[8] while von Galling divides it into thirty-seven sections dealing with as many varied theses and propositions.[9] As we have said there is no logical order here: the Preacher "thinks with the eye" and tells us what he sees "under the sun."

c) QOHELETH: EXPERIMENTS AND CONCLUSIONS

Now, to come to the Preacher himself. He is a unique

[7]H. W. Hertzberg, *Der Prediger* (1932).

[8]K. Budde, *Die Heitige Schriften des Alten Testament* (edited by Kautzsch), 4th edition (1923).

[9]K. Galling, *Die fünf Megilloth* (1940).

figure among the Sages for while these were more or less associated in a regular group, Ecclesiates seems to be a complete free-lance. He does not belong to the union. His thoughts are not their thoughts nor are his ways their ways. He is bound by no school and owes allegiance to no institution. He is distinct and singular and would probably have found difficulty in working with others: of this he seems to be quite conscious (4:9, 7:28). J. M. Devine entitles his book on Ecclesiates *Confessions of an Adventurous Soul* and certainly the Preacher was one who ventured far and lived dangerously in his search for truth. To him came many strange experiences and out of his varied spiritual pilgrimage he gave us this book. Here we have the confessions of an enquiring spirit. This man is going to make a clean breast of things.

Ecclesiastes has no interest in dogma unless it be to refute it. He raises no question as to the existence of God. That is a general characteristic of all Hebrew Wisdom. The Sages never approached their enquiries without theological presuppositions: they had no desire to investigate final causes. They started from the fundamental axiom, "In the beginning God," and this postulate indicates the character of their studies: these were not speculative but practical. Their desire was not so much to understand the works of God as to acquaint themselves with their harmonies, beauties, and adaptations, and all this with a view to knowing and doing the will of God. In that sense the Preacher is thoroughly Hebrew and thoroughly practical.

As he surveys life from every side and aspect of experience he finds man is powerless and weak and his best efforts come to nothing. There is something sad and somber in the terms the Preacher employs: *vanity* (thirty-two times), *labor and toil* (thirty-five times), *fate* (thirteen times). These terms recur with deadening monotony and fall upon our ears with the sound of clods falling on coffins. In 1:2 the word vanity (*chebel*) occurs five times in eight words: the Jew counts it seven times in eight words on the ground that the plural "vanities" represents more than one and ordains that the mourner returning from the grave must come to a stand seven separate times and pause to think of the fleetingness of life. *Chebel* (vanity) is the vapor or exhalation that comes from the body as seen on a cold day. So fleeting, transient, and insubstantial is life.

Ecclesiastes cannot but speak as to what he has seen and heard. He has experimented and right at the beginning he gives us his result, just as does the singer in Psalm 73, though here the result is altogether different. We set forth what he found in the following metrical form made in the style of Omar Khayyam by F. Crawford Burkitt (privately printed at Rouen in 1918):[10]

> Bubble of bubbles! All things are a Bubble!
> What is the use of all Man's toil and trouble?
> Year after year the Crop comes up and dies,
> The Earth remains, Mankind is only Stubble.
>
> The rising Sun will set and rise once more;
> The Wind goes roving round from Shore to Shore,
> From North to South it goes, and round and round,
> And back again to where it was before.
>
> All rivers run into the Sea we know,
> And yet the Sea doth never overflow
> Back to the place from whence their Waters came
> By unknown Channels must the Rivers go.
>
> The weary Round continues as begun,

[10]This translation is being used in these pages.

The Eye sees naught effective to be done,
   Nor does the ear hear aught to satisfy—
There's nothing, nothing, New under the Sun.

Something (they tell us) really New at last!
Why, surely, it was known in Ages past;
   The Memory has faded, that is all,
And all our Lore will vanish just as fast.

There is a monotony in Nature and in History that only terrifies and daunts men: it robs men of hope and deprives life of meaning. What can man do in face of this awful endless fact? That is the fundamental question for the Sage. Is life worth living? What profits it a man? *Ma yithron* (what profit) occurs in this or similar form thirteen times throughout the book: perhaps we Americans can understand that viewpoint better than most folk for our standards are largely utilitarian. It is not that the Preacher is deifying Natural Law: he may be agnostic but he is not atheistic. Unlike the Hebrews who normally looked on Nature as the vehicle of divine revelation (cp. Psalm 19) the Preacher here is intimidated by the machine-like regularity and deadly monotony of the natural processes. It overwhelms him and leaves him conscious of nothing but futility and impotence. It is the same idea as we find in A. E. Housman:

Yonder see the morning blink:
   The sun is up, and up must I,
To wash and dress and eat and drink
And look at things and talk and think
   And work, and God knows why.

Oh, often have I washed and dressed
   And what's to show for all my pain?
Let me lie abed and rest:

> Ten thousand times I've done my best
> And all's to do again.[11]

Ma yithron—what does it profit? What's to show for all my pain? There seems no difference between the pessimism of the Preacher and the pejorism of Housman, for a pejorist is one on the way to become a pessimist.

But Ecclesiastes will not despair. There is a frequently recurring phrase employed by the Preacher, "I turned and I saw" (4:7) or "I turned myself to behold" (2:12) which might well be translated "I took a second look." It is wise to look again, for on a first glance we may fail to see something vital. The Preacher will leave no experiment untried, no path untrod as he seeks to solve the riddle of the universe. Being an empiricist he tried various experiments. The first was with Wisdom and here he sought the way of intellectual ambition. A sore disappointment it was to him to find there was no profit here:

> I in Jerusalem was Israel's King;
> I set my mind to study everything
>   Under the Heavens, how God hath contrived
> That grievous Care men to their work should bring.
>
> I saw what was accomplished everywhere,
> And all was Bubble and a meal of Air;
>   That which comes short cannot be made enough,
> And what grows crooked Man can not make fair   (1:12–15)

All his advances here only made him more conscious of life's futility. Other experiments he must try and along the path of aesthetic delight and even on the road of coarse physical sensations he sought to attain his goal, but all in vain.

---

[11]"Yonder See the Morning Blink" from *Last Poems* by A. E. Housman. Copyright, 1922, by Henry Holt and Company, Inc., Copyright, 1950, by Barclays Bank, Ltd. Used by permission of the publishers. P. 110.

I told myself, More Wisdom I have gained
Than all that in Jerusalem have reigned;
    Wisdom and Folly both proved empty Air,
The more I knew, the more my Mind was pained.

I said, Then I'll put Pleasure to the Test,
And this was just a Bubble like the rest;
    Laughter seemed foolish, pointless was my Play,
Even in my Cups I kept in mind my Quest.

I looked at what my Wisdom had prepared,
In which some Folly too had partly shared,
    And when I thought upon my Heirs to be
I asked, Is Folly then with Wisdom paired?

I saw that Wisdom is the better state
As Light is better than the Dark, its Mate;
    The Wise Man's Eyes are in his Head, the Fool
Walks in the dark and recks not of his Fate.

But there's one Law no Wisdom can defy,
Though I be wise, I like the Fool must die;
    What Gain will then to me my Wisdom bring?
"This also is a Bubble," was my Cry.

(1:16–2:1–3, 13–16)

Knowledge and study did not satisfy. That is the more wonderful in that men of that time thought knowledge was the
key to success. It may have been that in his search he visited
the great library at Thebes which called itself, "the hospital
of the soul," and like Macbeth he may have asked:

Canst thou not minister to a mind diseased,
Pluck from the memory a rooted sorrow,
Raze out the written troubles of the brain,
And with some sweet oblivious antidote
Cleanse the stuff'd bosom of that perilous stuff
Which weighs upon the heart?

To which would come back the answer:

Therein the patient must minister to himself.

Words, words, words, and "of making many books there is
no end" (12:12). *Weltschmerz* is hard to heal and perhaps
only the Beatific Vision will suffice. But the Preacher could
not see beyond the bounds of time and sense; for him life
was untouched by "the scents and murmurs of the infinite
sea."

Nor could pleasure afford satisfaction. The life of the
sybarite was but a meal of air. This, too, is vanity

> But pleasures are like poppies spread,
> You seize the flower, its bloom is shed;
> Or like the snow-fall in the river,
> A moment white, then melts for ever.   (R. Burns)

The pursuit of beauty and the gratifications of sensual pleas-
ures were as unrewarding as the search for knowledge. All
alike were but a "Bubble and a Meal of Air."

The end result of these experiments and adventures is
expressed in the terrible words of 2:17, "and so I hated life."

> And so I hated Life; it seemed a Curse,
> All things under the Sun were so perverse,
>   All was a Bubble and a Meal of Air,
> And all my Wisdom had but made it worse.

> All I had done and all I had to do
> I hated leaving to No one knows Who,
>   One coming after me, perhaps as Wise,
> Perhaps a Fool—that was a Bubble, too!

> For what hath such a one his Profit in?
> A weary struggle all his Days have been,
>   Even in the Night his Mind had little rest,
> And what is his Reward? A Bubble thin!

> Surely the Worker should enjoy his Fill;
> It is not so: hath God, then, managed ill?

For who can think the ancient Adage true
That "God gives whom He chooses Craft and Skill,

But to the Sinner He gives Care and Zest
To toil and work to feather his own nest
For God to give to whom He chooses"?—Nay,
This is a thinner Bubble than the rest.   (2:17–19, 22–26)

There are two kinds of disappointment in life: there is
the disappointment of the man who has failed to attain his
goal and there is the disappointment of him who has attained
and is not satisfied with what it has brought. In the latter
instance the flowers have withered and the fire has burned
to ashes and all he can say is "I hated life." This is "the
sorrow of the world that worketh death." But the other sorrow leads to repentance unto life, for a man learns through
his disappointment to say, "It was good for me that I was
afflicted," and thus he passes from under the cloud to a place
that is luminous with God. In that light he sees clearly and
ceases to say, "Father, give me," and learns through his new-
found vision to say, "Father, make me." For we have not
proceeded thus far in reading this book without observing
what a large place is occupied by the first person pronoun
"I." The Preacher is suffering from "I" trouble. Life is centered in self: he is an egoist. In 2:1–11, in eleven short verses,
we find "I" no less than twenty times! And the name of God
is not found there at all! The only hope for such a life is that
it should cease to be self-centered and become God-cen-
tered. Furthermore, thirty-one times in the book we meet
the phrase "Under the sun": it is not good to be so much
out in the sun. It is good to pass at times under the cloud.
But the Preacher had no philosophy of the cloud.

This egoism may partly account for the despairing pessi-
mistic note in Ecclesiastes. He does not seem to have been

a companionable spirit, but he well knew the community instinct is implanted in human nature and that the two qualities of justice and philanthropy are the fundamental conditions of community life. The Stoics knew this well and sought by word and deed to realize this ideal. But Ecclesiastes was not a Stoic. He is conscious of the problems created by man's inhumanity to man. The wicked seem to triumph on every side: tyranny and brutality hold sway everywhere.

> I gazed upon the world of Men around;
> From every side welled up the mournful Sound
>   Of the Oppressed who weep and have no Friend,
> While their Oppressors thrive upon the ground.
>
> And so I praised the Dead of long ago
> As happier than the Living whom we know,
>   And happier he who never has been born
> To see the evil Work done here below.
>
> I noted with what pain Success is won—
> And what's Success, when all is said and done?
>   Getting the better of another Man—
> Just one more Bubble under the Sun.   (4:1-5)

Perhaps it was the general view of society or the sense of his own loneliness that kindled in him the desire for cooperation and community effort:

> I know of one with neither Child nor Wife,
> Whose days are spent in weary Toil and Strife,
>   His Eye unsated with his Wealth acquired:
> For whom doth he impoverish his Life?
>
> That surely is a Bubble, all must own,
> For Two are better than One all alone,
>   Then if he fall his Partner picks him up:
> The lonely Climber slips and still lies prone.   (4:8; 10)

But the Preacher did not have the creative energy to translate his noble sentiments into action. He seems also, as an aristocrat, to have felt a deep distrust of the masses: here, too, the results were but vanity (4:13–16).

Justice was far to seek. In that ancient world might was right. The times were sorely out of joint and life was reduced to a survival of the slickest:

> All things I've seen in these my Days of Bubble;
> Some Good men in their Goodness come to trouble,
>   Some of the Wicked still prolong their Days
> In Deeds of Wickedness and Dealing double.   (7:15)

> It's a big Bubble, ah! how often met,
> That Good men suffer what the Bad should get,
>   And Bad men get rewarded like the Good,
> Yet seeing such Injustice do not fret.   (8:14)

Perhaps there was a certain inevitability about all this. For the old order had passed: the city state was long since gone and the "four freedoms" were but a memory. Alexander the Great was in control and military colossi bestrode the earth. Nor did things improve under the Roman Empire, for all such imperial institutions destroy liberty and crush individuality. The emergence of creative personality under such conditions is well-nigh impossible, for all are subject to the whims and arbitrary dictates of the conqueror. A man may not call his soul his own. Not even the philosophers could be fooled on that point. All were gripped in the ring of iron necessity which men could refer to as Fate (*Heimarmene*) or Chance (*Tyche*) or, as indefinitely, the gods.

It is interesting here to note how Ecclesiastes refers to God. He does not use the personal name *Yahwe* but only the term *Elohim* which may well be translated Deity. It has a somewhat hollow sound here and seems only an echo from

the distant past. It does not appear to have any real content
or meaning: it certainly has not the sound we find in the
passionate cries of the Psalmist or the plaintive melodies of
Jeremiah. A great gulf lies between these and the Preacher.
To the latter God seems but an idea; to these others He was
a vital experience. And we are not surprised to find in this
book other words that seem to have as much or more significance, words like *miqreh* (chance), *cheleq* (lot, destiny),
pega' (accident). No other book of the Old Testament contains so many such expressions:

> The way of human Fate I've tried to sift
> And seen the Race not going to the Swift,
> > Neither the Battle to the Strong, nor yet
> To the Wise man Honour or splendid Gift.

> In Chance and Ill-luck everybody shares;
> Like Fish caught in the Nets, or Birds in snares,
> > So Men are taken, Wise and Fool alike,
> Suddenly by Misfortune unawares.   (9:11, 12)

The God of Ecclesiastes seems no more than the thought
of an impersonal, unfeeling world-government, somewhat
akin to M. Arnold's thought of a "Power, not ourselves, that
makes for righteousness." Ecclesiastes might have assented
to the thought of power but he would—and did—question
the thought of righteousness.

We may note here that Ecclesiastes appears to have lost
something that was characteristic of Hebrew thought and
piety in an earlier period. That piety was composed of two
elements that enabled men to see a harmony in the general
scheme of things. The two main elements in that piety were
1) an intense reverential awe (*pachad*) towards God and
2) a profound sense of intimacy and communion with the
same God. The immanent and the transcendent, "the near

God" and "the far God" were combined in Hebrew religious experience. To the Psalmist, Yahwe is clothed with honor and with majesty and exalted very high, "by terrible things in righteousness" He reveals Himself to men so that "they fear before Him." But He is also the gentle shepherd of Israel who draws nigh to the contrite spirit and hears and answers prayer. "The friendship of Yahwe is with them that fear Him" (Psalm 25:14) is a phrase defining the real nature of Hebrew religious experience. That experience of the saints is a sealed book to Ecclesiastes: we never see this Preacher on his knees at prayer. Words like forgiveness, grace, redemption, the fatherly nature of God—we need not look for such terms in this book. If the Preacher ever prayed he must have prayed in the weird words of the preacher referred to earlier (p. 12), "O Thou who art our great working hypothesis . . ." But one cannot commune with a hypothesis or cordialize with an *ens rationis* or cosmic principle. That is how this Preacher thought of God and the hypothesis does not appear to be vital to his thought. D. B. MacDonald is not wide of the mark when he writes:

> His relation to God was not in the least religious: it was at most theological, a recognition of God's existence as an absolutely controlling will behind life. And, indeed, he had set himself, using this fact and reality of life, to circumvent that absolute will.[12]

And yet again the same writer says:

> For Ecclesiastes life was good and living beings could be wise and kind, but that Being behind life was entirely amoral —wise, it might be, terribly wise.[13]

[12]D. B. MacDonald, *The Hebrew Philosophical Genius* (1936), p. 89.
[13]*Ibid.*, p. 137.

The main result of the loss of the Hebrew heritage was that Ecclesiastes had come to think of the Deity in terms of a despot before whom men must cringe in fear and abject submission. Thus Johannes Pedersen can say:

> That which characterises God is that he is not bound by any law: he acts in purely arbitrary fashion. Nothing comes to pass in the world which is not his work . . . but the annoying thing is that this divine activity is completely foreign to human and moral law. The essential motive of God is solely to maintain his absolute power and to make men feel, "God does this in order that men may fear him."[14]

And we can follow the same writer in his judgment:

> The Allah of Mohammed and the God of Qoheleth are very closely related.[15]

D. B. MacDonald perhaps pushes the matter too far when he says that Ecclesiastes[16] "was not interested in God except as a Being to be avoided" but the Preacher certainly did urge caution in any dealings with the Deity:

> Be not too Good, and be not Over-wise;
> Be not too Bad, the Fool's Cap is no Prize;
> Why die before thy Time? Try this and that—
> He who fears God will not be snared by lies.   (7:16,17)

The Preacher was familiar with the Greek ideal of moderation—*mēden agan*—and he knew of Epicurus and how the Greek philosopher preferred to have the gods mind their own business. But the Preacher was not too sure that they did just that. It was wiser to play safe. And though the Preacher makes no reference to the temple and its worship he does indicate the line of caution to be adopted here:

[14]*Ibid.*, p. 51.   [15]J. Pedersen, *op. cit.*, p. 43.   [16]*Op. cit.*, p. 141.

Be not rash with thy mouth nor be in a hurry to utter words before the Deity, for the Deity is in the skies and thou art on earth: therefore let thy words be few. When thou makest a vow to the Deity do not delay to fulfill it for "there is no pleasure in fools": what you vow be sure to fulfill. Better no vow at all than a vow without fulfillment.   (5:4, 5)

There is no use in playing with fire and it is better to be on the safe side. "Shut mouths catch no flies" and it will not avail to say to "the angel" (that is, the temple official) "It was a mistake" (5:5). The wise man will not run a risk.

What then are we to say? What can a man do? Let him eat drink and be merry for tomorrow he dies. *Carpe diem*— enjoy life while we may.

> Go eat in Cheerfulness thy daily Food,
> And drink thy Wine as an Immortal would.
>   Be well content, while yet thou canst enjoy,
> That God is pleased to let thee still see Good.
>
> Put off thy Mourning, give the rein to Mirth,
> Cherish thy Wife while yet thou art on Earth,
>   While yet thy Bubble lasts under the Sun—
> This is what God has judged thy Toil is worth.
>
> And whatso'er thine Hand shall find to try,
> Do it with all thy Might and Skill—for why?
>   There's neither Work nor Purpose, Craft or Thought
> Or Wisdom in the Grave, where thou wilt lie.   (9:7–10)

It may be that Ecclesiastes knew well the early stories in Genesis, but his view is not the view of the early writer. The latter is characterized by a healthy optimism that sees retrieval and redemption as the abiding purpose of God. The Preacher sees no such purpose in the scheme of things: he sees Paradise Lost but has no vision of Paradise Regained. His view of history is cyclical and circular, not linear and moving towards a consummation. He is impressed with the toil and futility of things: they go round and round but there is no movement forward and onward. There is no hope.

> God's Aim—how difficult it is to trace!
> I've seen Rogues sitting in the Judge's place,
> > The Bad man sits where Righteousness should be,
> And Merit stands before him in Disgrace.

> God lets the Wicked flourish; no doubt He
> Will judge them justly, but it seems to me
> > That He has made Men for Experiment
> To try what kind of Animals they be.   (3:16–18)

Surely this is the worm's-eye view of the world. Had not he heard of "man made in the image of God"? Did he not believe man was more than animal? To the Preacher there was no difference;

> For one Event comes both to Man and Beast,
> There's no Distinction when the Breath has ceased;
> > As one does, so the other—Bubbles both,
> And Man nowise superior in the least.   (3:19)

It may be that at this time a discussion had been going on as to this point. Has man a spirit (*ruach*) different from that of the beast?—the Old Testament attributes breath, spirit, wind, (*ruach*) to both man and beast. Where was the difference? Some seem to have argued that at death the *ruach* (spirit) of man goes upward while the *ruach* of the beast goes downward. The Preacher will have none of this:

> Who knows the Breath of Man is upward bound,
> While the Beast's Breath sinks downward to the Ground?
> > Out of the Dust we came, to Dust we go:
> All things return to tread the unchanging Round.   (3:20, 21)

Only life remains and let a man make all he may of that:

So I see nothing Better can be got
Than Work and taking Pleasure in our Lot:
  For who can ever show us what will come
After us, whether it be Good or not.   (3:22)

Not that he longs for death, nor will he, like the Stoic, seek
an exodus from the prison-house of life by suicide: he shud-
ders at the nothingness of death:

He who yet lives, there still is Hope for him,
For living Dogs more than dead Lions grim:
  The Living know that they will die at last,
The Dead know nothing, all to them is dim.

Their Memory is past, their Race is run,
Their Love, their Hate, their Rivalry is done,
  No Part nor Lot have they for evermore
In all the Work of Men under the Sun.   (9:4-6)

If in this world only we have hope, then are we of all men
most miserable. It is a melancholy picture we get from the
Preacher:

A melancholy Picture, Line by Line,
Howe'er we deck it out in Phrases fine:
  It shows Man going to his long, long Home,
The Funeral Procession, yours and mine.

That is the end of all the Toil and Trouble:
To Earth goes back once more the Dust and Rubble,
  The Breath returns again to God who gave—
Bubble of Bubbles! All things are a Bubble.   (12:7)

d) HOW CAN WE CLASSIFY THE PREACHER?

This strange book has left men wondering how to classify
the author. Some have thought to call him a Sadducee and
there are elements in his teaching that seem close to those
of Sadducean doctrine—his interest in political life, his de-

tached attitude to the religious cult, and his negative viewpoint in relation to the future life. But the Preacher is not a Sadducee: he is a strict determinist and the Sadducees were certainly not that. Is he a Pharisee? or an Essene? The Pharisees believed in partial determinism (synergism) while the Essenes were wholly given to asceticism. No Pharisee, surely, ever spoke like Ecclesiastes and certainly the Preacher had no place for ascetic rites:

> Put away Sorrow, have thy Heart's Delight,
> Practice no Hardship or ascetic Rite,
>> But think from whence thou art, and whither bound,
> Before the Evil Days come on thee quite;
>
> The Days when thou wilt say "I do not care,"
> When all the Light of Heaven will seem less fair,
>> Days without Sunshine, when, the Summer past,
> The Clouds still gather in the murky Air.   (11:9, 10)

We cannot label the Preacher with any Jewish affiliation. He refuses to be classified with the current categories.

Nor may he be classified with a Greek label. He has been called a Stoic and elements of Stoicism are here; in lesser degree we may find elements of Epicurus. Pyrrho, the founder of the Sceptical School, has been regarded as contributing to the Preacher's thought, while others have found his apparent sources in Hesiod or Theognis. All these elements are present because they were present and potent in the world of that time. Such ideas in the form of an amalgam constituted the general *milieu* of Ecclesiastes' time. Such ideas floated around and were on people's lips in the same sort of amalgam as was found later at Ephesus in the days of the early church.

Ecclesiastes defies classification. He is wholly *sui generis*, a unique and distinct personality. In personal characteristics and outlook he is perhaps most akin to Marcus Aurelius, but he is still himself and not another. He was distinct and distinguished enough to give rise to a kind of school or group of devotees who later attracted the attention of *Ecclesiasticus* and the author of the *Wisdom of Solomon*. To Jerome the book commended itself as a manual enjoining world-renunciation, while to Comenius it appealed as a book of consolation. To Frederick the Great it seemed the most precious book in the Bible, while Renan, as already indicated, judged it the most lovable book written by a Jew. We may think of it, however, as valuable for another reason. It represents what comes to a man who has lost his moorings in ancestral piety and has not found a point of rest in any new satisfying system. It shows how the thought of the absolute nothingness of human effort must lead in the fullness of time to the thought of a new creation.

> Ecclesiastes, like the first part of Goethe's Faust, may, with the fullest justice, be called an apology for Christianity, not as containing anticipations of Christian truth . . . but inasmuch as it shows that neither Wisdom nor any other human good or pleasure brings permanent satisfaction to man's natural longings.[17]

Ecclesiastes represents the bankruptcy of human thinking and the barrenness of egoism. Egoism had to give place to altruism and selfishness had to make way for service. In that sense the book is a *Praeparatio evangelica* and Hertzberg may be right in his opinion that here we have one of the most startling Messianic predictions.[18]

[17]T. K. Cheyne, *Job and Solomon,* p. 249.
[18]*Op. cit.*

IX

Wisdom in the Psalter

WE PASS FROM the book of Ecclesiastes to the Psalter and the passing is like passing from a desert into a land flowing with milk and honey. Here we come to "the King's Gardens" where are all manner of pleasant fruits and beauteous flowers. Here we enter the fellowship of the Saints and we sit down with them in the spacious banqueting house where His banner over us is love and His fruit is sweet to our taste.[1]

a) THE VITAL SENSE OF GOD

Here God becomes real and vital. "The friendship of the Lord is with him that fear him" (Psalm 25:14) and we come to understand that deep sense of communion with the living God that could express itself in such variegated imagery as it speaks of God as shield and buckler, a strong tower into which men run as the conies run into the clefts of the rock, a refuge and defence and hiding-place—so near is God, "closer than breathing, nearer than hands or feet." And yet also so far and high, riding on the clouds, inhabiting eternity, sitting in the heavens, commanding the earth from the rising of the sun even to the going-down of the same—such is the Psalmist's thought of God. And the near God and the far God become one God in the experience of the adoring wor-

[1]See also the author's *The Praises of Israel* (1950).

shipper, for the great God who numbers the stars is the good God who heals the broken heart and binds up the wounds of His children (Psalm 143:3, 4). For the true worshipper, there is no contrast between the splendors of the God who rules on high and the tenderness of Him who

> With scarce an intervention presses close
> And palpitatingly, His soul o'er ours.[2]

Dwelling in the heavens He nonetheless makes the humble heart and the contrite spirit His dwelling-place: man is known of God and constrained to praise Him:

> How precious also are thy thoughts unto me, O God!
> How great is the sum of them!
> If I should count them, they are more in number than the sand:
> When I awake, I am still with thee.   (Psalm 139:17, 18)

This is the sheer wonder of life and the living God that was hid from the eyes of the Preacher.

Nor is it otherwise in regard to the Psalmist's attitude to the temple, the place where God's honor dwelleth. Did Ecclesiastes frequent its courts or feel drawn to the shrine? Wild horses could not have kept the Psalmist away from Mount Zion.

> How lovely is thy dwelling-place,
>   O Lord of hosts, to me!
> The tabernacles of thy grace
>   how pleasant, Lord, they be.
>
> My thirsty soul longs veh'mently:
>   yea faints, thy courts to see:
> My very heart and flesh cry out,
>   O living God, for thee.[3]   (Psalm 84:1, 2)

[2]Cited from W. T. Davison, *The Praises of Israel* (1902), p. 122.
[3]The version here is the Metrical Version approved by the Church of Scotland and appointed to be used in Worship: Oxford University Press.

No joy equalled the joy of the Psalmist as he went up to
that temple that drew the pilgrims from afar:

> I joy'd when to the house of God,
>   Go up, they said to me.
> Jerusalem, within thy gates
>   our feet shall standing be . . .
>
> Pray that Jerusalem may have
>   peace and felicity:
> Let them that love thee and thy peace
>   have still prosperity . . .
>
> Now, for my friends' and brethren's sakes
>   Peace be in thee, I'll say.
> And for the house of God our Lord,
>   I'll seek thy good alway.   (Psalm 122:1, 6, 8, 9)

There is a strange weight of passion in these songs: the
temple and its ministries linger with the pilgrim like remembered music.

That is the vast gulf that yawns between the temper of
the Preacher and the devotion of the Psalter. One star dif-
fereth from another in glory and to each is given varied
gifts and other graces.

In form some of the Wisdom of the Psalter is not unlike
that found in the book of Proverbs. But there can be no mistaking the difference in substance. The short pithy sayings
of Proverbs are formally matched in the words of the Psalter
but none can fail to feel the difference in spiritual intensity.
Let us look at an example.

> Except the Lord build the house,
>   they labor in vain that build it:
> Except the Lord keep the city,
>   the watchman waketh *but* in vain.   (Psalm 127:1)

Look at this thought as expressed in Proverbs:

> The horse is prepared against the day of battle:
>> but safety is of the Lord.   (Proverbs 21:31)

The first has the sound of an ultimatum: it has the urgency of life and death. The latter is a generalization and leaves us almost unmoved. It is small wonder that noble families have chosen this saying for inscription on their family crest and that noble cities like Edinburgh have made it their motto and principle of life while builders of beneficent edifices like Eddystone lighthouse built it into their work and inscribed it on the stone. For it touches the roots and realities of things and constitutes the only real foundation for the good life. We may pursue this same Psalm a little further and find this wise word:

> Lo, children are an heritage of the Lord,
> *And* the fruit of the womb *is his* reward.
> As arrows are in the hand of a mighty man;
> So *are* the children of the youth.
> Happy *is* the man that hath his quiver full of them:
> They shall not be ashamed but they shall speak
> With the enemies in the gate.   (Psalm 127:3–5)

Civilizations, ancient and modern, have fallen and bitten the dust for failure to heed this word. Proverbs knew it, too, but could not shape to the lively form of the Psalm:

> Children's children are the crown of old men;
> And the glory of children are their fathers.   (Proverbs 17:6)

Ecclesiastes knew from sad experience the high worth of the social bond that binds a man to his fellows (Ecclesiastes 4:9) but the Psalmist expresses it with a lyric beauty that was inaccessible to the Preacher:

> Behold, how good a thing it is,
>> and how becoming well,

> Together such as brethren are
> > in unity to dwell!

> Like precious ointment on the head,
> > that down the beard did flow,
> Ev'n Aaron's beard and to the skirts
> > did of his garments go.

> As Hermon's dew, the dew that doth
> > on Sion' hills descend;
> For there the blessing God commands,
> > life that shall never end.   (Psalm 133)

Clearer, too, and more concrete is the Psalter in the setting forth of life's alternatives. Madame Wisdom and Madame Folly are somewhat elusive figures and are not as clearly discerned as the High Road and the Low Road of Psalm 1. The "Two Ways" are known to all and every mother's son must travel one or the other. Religion to the Hebrew was walk rather than talk: a "way" was something very clear and definite, so clear and definite that not even "a fool could err therein" (Isaiah 35:8). The Godly and the Ungodly stand clearly limned and stand over against each other as do the Wise Man and the Fool in Proverbs. But in the Psalter we have a more religious atmosphere: the aim is the good life. Proverbs deals with man's mind, but the Psalmist aims at the heart and the emotions. Its characteristic note and emphasis can be seen in such a passage as Psalm 119:9–14:

> By what means shall a young man learn
> > his way to purify?
> If he according to thy word
> > thereto attentive be.

> Unfeignedly thee have I sought
> > with all my soul and heart:
> O let me not from the right path
> > of thy commands depart.

Thy word I in my heart have hid,
    that I offend not thee.
O Lord, thou ever blessed art,
    thy statutes teach thou me.

The judgments of thy mouth each one
    my lips declared have;
More joy thy testimonies' way
    than riches all me gave.

I will thy holy precepts make
    my meditation;
And carefully I'll have respect
    unto thy ways each one.

Upon thy statutes my delight
    shall constantly be set;
And, by thy grace, I never will
    thy holy word forget.

This used to be a favorite passage in the religious education of youth and in Scotland aforetime young children were taught to commit it to memory. And where could they get anything more worthy and salutary?

b) DOUBTS AND UNCERTAINTIES

But life to the Psalmist was frequently darkened with doubt and uncertainty. The mood of gloom frequently appears and man's faith has to be asserted in face of hostile circumstance, for to those ancient singers life was limited by time and space and the ways of God with men were not always clear. The presence and power of wicked men constituted a real problem for the Psalmist who held the current and contemporary doctrine of divine recompense. The wicked man sharpened his tongue like a razor and devised evil upon his bed and with the morning light proceeded to execute his cruel purposes (Psalms 36, 52). And too often he succeeded in making life intolerable for the righteous whose earnest cry and prayer ceased not to ascend before God. "How long, O Lord, how long?" is the burden of that cry, for the faith of the Psalmist was strong and he believed it was but a question of time:

> How long, O Lord, wilt thou forget me for ever?
> How long wilt thou hide thy face from me?
> How long shall I keep anxious cares in my soul,
>   *Having* sorrow in my heart daily?
> How long shall mine enemy be exalted over me?
>
> (Psalm 13:1, 2)

These words were often on the lips of John Calvin but faith did not fail, for he believed with the saints of old that though weeping may endure for a night joy cometh with the morn. And one arose after another to say:

> This poor man cried and the Lord heard *him,*
> and saved him out of all his troubles.   (Psalm 34:6)

Experience, national and individual, fortified faith. And if, as scholars now maintain, those great redemptive acts were continually renewed and made visible in dramatic form in the religious cult we need not be surprised at this continuous upsurge of confident faith. We may pass for a moment to a psalm outside the Psalter to hear the glowing expression of this faith. The psalm is found in the book of Habakkuk who was vexed by the riddle of the universe:

> What though no flow'rs the fig-tree clothe,
>   though vines their fruit deny,
> The labour of the olive fail,
>   and fields no meat supply?
>
> Though from the fold, with sad surprise,
>   my flock cut off I see;

Though famine pine in empty stalls,
    where herds were wont to be?

Yet in the Lord will I be glad,
    and glory in his love;
In Him I'll joy, who will the God
    of my salvation prove.

He to my tardy feet shall lend
    the swiftness of the roe;
Till, rais'd on high, I safely dwell
    beyond the reach of woe.

God is the treasure of my soul,
    the source of lasting joy;
A joy which want shall not impair,
    nor death itself destroy.
        (Habakkuk 3:17, 18 Scots Paraphrase)

That is as lyrical and triumphant as Saint Paul himself in his great shout:

> Who shall separate us from the love of Christ? *Shall* tribulation, or distress, or persecution, or famine, or nakedness, or peril, or sword? . . . Nay, in all these things we are more than conquerors through him that loved us.   (Romans 8:35, 37)

That is the mood of the Psalter as it marks the joy of that ancient worshipper as he beholds anew in the cult the wondrous works of his God and finds his faith strengthened by the vision.

But the question "Why?" is more pressing than the question "How long?" And in the Psalter we meet the question as it emerged in the book of Job, for the theology of Job and his friends is the theology of the Psalter. Piety should bring prosperity and suffering should be the portion of evildoers. But the Psalmist saw that life did not always work that way, and the insurgent "Why?" arose. Nor need we wonder that it should be so or that the cry of the singer should be so clamant at times, for in this life alone he had hope. There was, normally, no thought of life hereafter:

> In death there is no remembrance of thee:
> in the grave who shall give thee thanks?   (Psalm 6:5)

> What profit is there in my blood when I go down
>   to the Pit?
>   Shall the dust praise thee? shall it declare thy
>   truth?   (Psalm 30:9)

> Wilt thou show wonders to the dead?
> Shall the dead arise and praise thee?
> Shall thy lovingkindness be declared in the grave?
> *or* thy faithfulness in destruction?
> Shall thy wonders be known in the dark?   4
> and thy righteousness in the land of forgetfulness?
>   (Psalm 88:10–12)

The wistful pathos of these words indicates how somber life is to those without a future hope and their frequent repetition, as in Job, shows the depth of man's longing for such a sure hope.

Psalm 37 deals with the problem of innocent suffering, but we feel there is a certain unreality in the treatment of the question. Its assertions fly in the face of the facts of life:

> Fret not thyself because of evildoers,
> Neither be thou envious against the workers
>   of iniquity.
> For they shall soon be cut down like the grass,
> And wither as the green herb.
> Trust in the Lord, and do good;
> So shalt thou dwell in the land,
> And verily thou shalt be fed.   (Psalm 37:1–3)

Here we have the current theology of that period stated and the singer believes it accords with the facts of life:

> I have been young and now am old;
> Yet have I not seen the righteous forsaken,
> Nor his seed begging bread.   (Psalm 37:25)

Had he never heard of Job? Was he unacquainted with the undeniable fact of the sufferings of the righteous? Did he not see "the humble and the afflicted" who waited patiently for the Lord? We may admire the man's courage but his conclusion does not seem to rest on adequate examination of the facts.

c) GLEAMS OF GLORY

Psalm 49 tackles the problem more manfully. It recognizes the prosperity of the wicked and it does not deny the suffering of the innocent. The rich ride high and fare sumptuously every day: they have cities called after them and are buried with fulsome eulogies in magnificent mausoleums. That is how it seems to end, but is it really so? The singer views the whole question against the background of death. Yes, that is the end—for them. Death feeds on them and all is over. They have nothing to look forward to. But the Psalmist has:

> But God will redeem my soul from the power of the grave:
> For he shall receive me.   (Psalm 49:15)

God will not forsake his saints. He is faithful: he is just. The word "receive" is an eschatological term and is the term used with reference to God's dealing with Enoch:

> And Enoch walked with God, and he was not: for God took him.   (Genesis 5:24)

The same word is used of the translation of Elijah (II Kings

2:9, 10). The writer is here saying death is not the end for the righteous: There is something more to come. Many interpreters refuse to give this wider reference to these words, but the meaning here is plain to see: there is a life hereafter for the righteous. Such a thought may be expressed in Psalm 16:10, 11:

> For thou wilt not leave my soul in Sheol:
> neither wilt thou suffer thine holy one to see corruption.
>
> Thou wilt shew me the path of life:
> in thy presence is fulness of joy;
> at thy right hand there are pleasures for evermore.

This may not be as clear as Psalm 49:15 and it may be open to another interpretation as is also Psalm 17:15:

> As for me, I will behold thy face in righteousness:
> I shall be satisfied, when I awake, with thy likeness.

It is possible that these words may be interpreted without reference to life hereafter but this does not seem possible in the case of Psalm 49:15. As to when the idea of life hereafter or resurrection arose among the Hebrews there is difference of opinion. It was late in Judaism before we find clear expressions on the question. The Apocalyptic section in Isaiah (Isaiah 24–27) is usually dated not earlier than the second century B.C. and there we find the thought clearly expressed. We give this as translated by G. B. Gray in the *International Critical Commentary* on Isaiah:

> Thy dead shall live,
>> Their corpses shall arise;
>> They that dwell in the dust,
>> Shall awake and give a ringing cry.
> For the dew of . . . is thy dew,
>> And the earth shall give birth to shades.
>
> (Isaiah 26:19)

Or let us look at another passage whose date cannot be later than 165 B.C.—the passage in Daniel 12:2 which reads thus:

> And many of them that sleep in the dust of the earth shall awake, some to everlasting life, and some to shame and everlasting contempt.

Quite obviously this idea has grown in Daniel (165 B.C.) beyond the thought of Psalm 49:15 and that is as we should expect. The idea did not spring full-blown like Athena from the head of Zeus. It has its faint anticipations in an earlier period and if T. H. Robinson was able to find the Greek idea of immortality in Job 19:25 f., we need not hesitate to find in the Psalter men groping and seeking this certainty. And always, be it noted, this assurance rises in connection with human suffering. It rises like a moral postulate which at the same time asserts the rights of moral personality and vindicates the righteousness of God.

All this becomes clearer when we look at Psalm 73. For here our evidence is cumulative. In Psalm 73 the singer tells us how he was sorely baffled with the apparent riddle of the universe. If there is a good and righteous God controlling this world, why do so many moral anomalies appear? Why should arrogant boastful men strut about in loud-mouthed pride and deride the very idea of a righteous God and a moral purpose in life? God is not in all their thoughts: they are clothed in fine linen and, like Dives, fare sumptuously every day while waters of a bitter cup are wrung out to God's saints. The man is about to give up religion altogether: "my steps had well nigh slipped," he tells us, and he was ready to deny the spiritual values of life. But God will not forsake His saints nor try them beyond endurance: He will not suffer the bleak black hour to overwhelm the heart that puts its

trust in Him. He touches man's weakness with His almighti
ness and sets man's feet upon a rock and gives the satisfying vision that enables man to see to the center of things and
know the truth:

> Nevertheless, I am continually with thee:
> Thou hast holden me by my right hand.
> Thou shalt guide me with thy counsel
> And afterward receive me to glory.
> Whom have I in heaven but thee?
> And there is none upon earth that I desire
>   beside thee.
> My flesh and my heart faileth:
> But God is the strength of my heart,
> And my portion for ever.   (Psalm 73:23–26)

That word "Nevertheless" is just one little letter in the original Hebrew, but it contains a world of argument. Luther
did not fail to discern its dimensions and the English translators followed in the same insight. It is a word of triumph
like Paul's "I know . . . and am persuaded." It signifies that
the man has seen through the things of time to the abiding
and eternal realities. And the heart is satisfied, as the heart
of Job was satisfied, with the vision. It means that he has
glimpsed the real character of God and knows that God is
Love, that Love is stronger than Death, and that to have
formed a friendship with God is to have fashioned a bond
which Death cannot break or annul. To mention Death here
is a sheer irrelevance and impertinence. God is stronger than
the strong man armed and none shall pluck His loved ones
from His almighty hands. Though all nature should give way
beneath our feet, He will hold us up and carry us through
the last cold river and establish us in the judgment. And all
the trumpets shall sound for us on the other side. That is the

Psalmist's assured confidence which nothing in earth or heaven can shake. God is more than all that be against us. God is just and God is merciful.

This may not constitute a doctrine of immortality. But no sound doctrine of immortality can be framed that does not rest on that deep assurance. As to how it will come to pass the writer does not say: the manner of his "taking" he leaves to God. Again we note the use of the eschatological terms, "glory," "take (receive)," and "afterward," all which terms are used regularly with reference to man's final destiny.

We may not leave this matter here: these are foregleams of glory. What happened when the fulness of light was given in Christ? Does he not build on this foundation?

d) THE NEW TESTAMENT FULFILLMENT

In the New Testament we find this teaching clearly and explicitly set forth. Look at the Gospel of Luke (20:27 f.) where certain Sadducees who did not believe in life hereafter seek to put Jesus on record in regard to this question. Through the hypothetical case of a woman married and widowed seven times they seek to show the absurdity of the idea of life hereafter. But they are "hoist with their own petard" as Jesus shows that they know not the real nature of spiritual life nor do they know their own Law. If they would but take time to read the story of Moses they would learn:

> Now that the dead are raised, even Moses showed at the Bush, when he called the Lord the God of Abraham, and the God of Isaac, and the God of Jacob. For he is not the God of the dead, but of the living: for all live unto him.
>
> (Luke 20:37, 38)

The meaning of that word was not grasped by those to whom Jesus spoke: it frequently takes time to comprehend a saying of such large import. But it did become very clear in the light of later events. What Jesus says here is that Abraham, the Friend of God and Father of the Faithful, is still God's friend and that death made no difference to that friendship. It was a friendship which death was impotent to break. Abraham and Isaac and Jacob are not "has-beens" swept away in the stream of time. The Syrian stars are not looking down on their graves: they look down on the Syrian stars. They stand in His presence and "serve him day and night in his temple."

Men could not understand such teaching then but it became very clear in the light of Christ's Resurrection. The disciples could put two and two together and finally reach a triumphant conclusion. But not immediately. After the death on Calvary we see the sheer despair of the disciples. "We used to hope that it had been he who should redeem Israel" (Luke 24:21). That seems far, far away like a distant echo. Hope had died; here we have the acme of disappointment and despair. Then something happened that transformed everything: the atmosphere of the Gospel story here becomes electric and men and women are running about shouting: "He is risen: we have seen Him." The Gospel stories become incoherent at this point and we cannot see clearly how it all happened. But we see the early Christian Church and a multitude leaping and dancing and praising God. All theology here is transformed into doxology so that the New Testament becomes the most radiant hymnbook ever written. What does all this mean? They had to explain it and here we meet the first Christian Apologetic. Listen to what they say:

It was not possible that he should be holden of death.
(Acts 2:24)

That is how Peter speaks and Paul is not saying otherwise when he says:

Death hath no more dominion over him.   (Romans 6:9)

They are recalling the teaching of our Lord in the days of his flesh and they are putting all the pieces together to solve this seeming riddle. Now they see what Jesus meant by that word on Abraham, Isaac, and Jacob and they see what is involved. They recall that radiant faith of his that cast itself in utter surrender on the love of the Father, that life which moved in absolute reciprocity with the Divine so that it was his "meat to do the will of Him that sent me" (John 4:34). They recalled that and they remembered the omnipotent love of God that was revealed in him: they thought these two facts together and they spoke as they were guided by the Holy Spirit. And that is what they said. For they knew now in the light of the central fact of the Resurrection that love omnipotent could not suffer defeat and that faith so complete and full could not fail of its reward. They were persuaded with a mighty persuasion that

neither death nor life, nor angels, nor principalities, nor powers, nor things present, nor things to come, nor height, nor depth, nor any other creature, shall be able to separate us from the love of God, which is in Christ Jesus our Lord.
(Romans 8:37, 38)

Faith such as that of Abraham who went out at the call of God, "not knowing whither he went" (Hebrews 11:8), had in itself the guarantee of immortality. Let us say it with all reverence: God would be unworthy to be called the God of trusting men if He were to leave such faith in the lurch. God could not afford to disappoint their adoring trust and surrender. And He does not, for as the writer of the Epistle to the Hebrews finely says:

God is not ashamed to be called their God. (Hebrews 11:16)

God meets the challenge and meets it with triumphant love. He is the God and Father of our Lord Jesus Christ.

That means for us that the New Testament writers base their thought of immortality—or better, life hereafter—on the nature of faith and the revealed character of God, which is precisely what Jesus had done. It is the faint gleam that first appeared in the book of Job and the Psalmists now shining as a radiant certainty. "He hath brought life and immortality to light" (II Timothy 1:13). And the doctrine here is mainly a truth of experience: it is not dogmatic but empirical. "The heart has reasons which the reason does not know" (Pascal). And when our doctrine is so grounded it will rest on twin pillars which may not easily be shaken.

We may add one word more. The Old Testament horizon as we have seen was limited; the New Testament prospect is boundless. There was reason for the Old Testament view that it should have its good things now: it could not afford to wait. The New Testament, however, could afford to wait for it saw beyond the veil and life here became one with life hereafter. Suffering, therefore, could be interpreted in another fashion and viewed in another light. It could be set *sub specie aeternitatis* and man could see clearly to the other side of his sorrow. In the light of that prospect the sufferings of the present time were nothing "compared to the glory that shall be revealed" (Romans 8:18). Thus the way of the Cross becomes the pathway to the Crown, for if we share in the fellowship of his sufferings we shall surely share in the fellowship of his glory.

Thus we can complete the saying of Lord Bacon and say that, while Prosperity is the blessing of the Old Testament, the blessing of the New Testament is Adversity.

> Blessed are ye, when men shall revile you and persecute you . . . rejoice, and be exceeding glad; for great is your reward in heaven. (Matthew 5:11, 12)

Thus the New Testament unfolds and makes explicit what is implicit in the Old Testament and both views rest on "the ultimate decency of things." Both are grounded in the eternal righteousness and love of God.

X

The Bible and Modern Life

WE HAVE BEEN OCCUPIED in the preceding chapters with various aspects of Life and Thought in the Old Testament. In this final chapter we wish to take a wider view and consider the Bible and Modern Life, for sometimes we are so busy looking at the trees that we miss the wood itself. Here we will try to "view all the land."

a) WHAT IS THE BIBLE?

The very word "Bible" suggests the East, for that word is derived from Byblos, the modern Gebal, one of the ancient cities of Syria and Palestine. Byblos was an important center for the Egyptian *papyrus,* whence through the Latin we get our word *paper.* From Byblos the Greeks called papyrus *biblos* and from that we get the form *biblion* (with its plural form *biblia*) meaning a book. The Latin took over the form *biblia* from the Greek and later this plural form was mistaken for a feminine singular noun: through this form which entered into English we get such forms as *bibil, bubil,* and later *bible.*

When we open the covers of the Bible recently published we find the title there:

The Holy Bible, containing the Old and New Testaments, translated from the original tongues being the version set

> forth A.D. 1611, revised A.D. 1881–1885 and A.D. 1901, com-
> pared with the most ancient authorities and revised A.D. 1952.

That is full and sonorous and might well impress us if we only stopped to think of what is here. For the very title breathes romance, suggesting, as it does, far-off Eastern lands and men and manners of other times. It speaks, too, of the loving care and preservation of the text which has been transmitted by "those most ancient authorities" to our own time. And it tells us that the Bible finds itself at home in East or West, and that time does not make its "ancient good uncouth."

It may help here to consider the Westminster divines who functioned in council shortly after the Authorized Version was made in 1611. They may help to clarify the title of the book.

The present writer was reared on the *Westminster Shorter Catechism* which was a concise manual of theology that supplied all the answers to all the questions with Scripture proofs to boot! This was absorbed into the system of the child before he reached the tender age of twelve. Doubtless many will snort at this method of teaching and it may be those snorters are justified in their snorting. From a pedagogical viewpoint such procedure was all wrong but fortunately educators in those days were not too much concerned with pedagogical principles. John Dewey had not yet arrived on the scene and Progressive Education was unknown. Moral and religious instruction was the aim of the schools and the *Shorter Catechism* and the Bible were the means and instruments of such instruction. It may reward us here to think of this as it yields a suitable starting point for our discussion.

The first question of the Catechism asked, "What is man's chief end?" to which was given the answer, "Man's chief end is to glorify God and to enjoy him for ever." Proceeding on their pedagogical path the divines asked, "What rule hath God given to direct us how we may glorify and enjoy him?" to which question came the fitting answer, "The Word of God which is contained in the Scriptures of the Old and New Testaments, is the only rule to direct us how we may glorify and enjoy him." And lest this might not be plain to the minds of childhood the divines proceeded to make things very clear with the third question, "What do the Scriptures principally teach?" to which the answer was, "The Scriptures principally teach, what man is to believe concerning God, and what duty God requires of man." The Westminster divines did not fail to make clear what they understood the Bible to be: it was "the only rule of faith" and it was a source of doctrine. It was intended as a manual of instruction. In this they were not much different from the Sages of Israel.

That is the view of the Bible which most of us have inherited. Whether it is a right and adequate view remains to be seen. For when we begin to study the Bible we are forced to the admission that if it was intended to be a manual of instruction it is strangely designed for such a purpose. It certainly does not conform to our ideas of what such a manual should be. If we had to construct a textbook with the declared purpose of the Westminister divines it would certainly be a book quite different from the Bible we have. We would expect such a book to begin with a definition of God and we would look for a full discussion of the moral and metaphysical attributes of Deity. We would further seek a comprehensive body of religious truth wherein would be set forth clearly the relations of God and man with a due concern for the restraint and correction of any vicious tendencies in human nature. Such a book, too, should contain a complete and consistent scheme of doctrine and it should not fail to afford complete guidance to the children of men by a clear revelation of the moral law. Not only should it give us clear ideas about God and unambiguous counsel as to our behavior but it should possess in rich measure such qualities as stir religious emotion. Something such as this we would expect a Bible to be but it has pleased God to give us something wholly otherwise. Clearly His thoughts are not our thoughts nor are His ways our ways: they may not even be the ways of the Westminster divines.

b) ITS CONCERN WITH LIFE AND LIVING

Let us look at this more closely. When we open the Bible and begin to read we find ourselves in a world of wonder. This seems altogether another world than ours. Here we have old world stories of the Garden of Eden, of God walking and talking and dining with men, tall tales like the Tower of Babel and Noah's flood: all this leaves us somewhat cold and unresponsive. Eleven times in Genesis we read, "these are the generations of . . ." and it would seem as if there were here nothing more than a family register. "Hatches, matches, and despatches" occupy most of the record and here is the story of one man's family followed through many generations. They live, they die, and are gathered to their fathers.

Nor is there much change as we continue to read. The journeyings of some Semitic tribes from Egypt to Canaan, their settlement in that land, the stories of kings and little kingdoms that were but pawns in the great game of international politics played by the great empires of the Near East—these are told in full detail. Great historical events of world significance are dismissed with a passing reference or not mentioned at all. The battle of Karkar in 853 B.C. is not mentioned: Alexander the Great and Julius Cæsar are not named. Luke is unique among the Bible writers in setting the story of Christ in the frame of world history. But the ancient writer will not fail to tell us that Eglon, king of Moab, was fat to an unseemly degree (Judges 3:22) and that Asa had gouty feet (II Chronicles 16:12) and that Jezebel "painted her face and attired her head" before she was rudely thrown out of the palace window and "some of her blood was sprinkled on the wall, and on the horses" (II Kings 9:30). The little coat that Samuel's mother made for him might seem insignificant beside his "linen ephod" but the ancient writer did not feel that way. Nor will he fail to tell us that Elisha was bald and little liked to be reminded of that fact (II Kings 2:23). There may not be too much divinity in all these stories, but there is a great deal of humanity. The writers were interested in life—common life. It may be that the Seers and the Sages bring us nearer to what we would expect a Bible to be: those austere stern Prophets who proclaim the judgment of God and those Wise Men who discuss the problems of life in a spirit of high seriousness and seek to direct men in the path of moral rectitude—these correspond more closely to our expectation.

Nor is it otherwise with the New Testament. Here we have simple narratives springing from the life of common folk and of Jesus who moved as a man among men. The beautiful stories of his birth at Bethlehem, the words of grace and truth that fell from his lips, the story of his Passion and Death—these will not cease to grip and hold men. The Epistles resemble more the prophetic writings for in these we see the church and its leaders endeavoring to regulate the life of the empire by Christian principles. But beyond one or two ambiguous references Jesus is not mentioned in Roman history: the land in which he lived seemed insignificant and Israel played a very minor role in the traffic and commerce of that ancient world.

Lest anyone should think we are exaggerating this vital element in Scripture let us listen to Sir Arthur Quiller-Couch who calls attention to the strange form of the Bible by asking us to imagine

> a volume including the great books of our own literature all bound together in such order as this: *Paradise Lost*, Darwin's *Descent of Man*, the *Anglo-Saxon Chronicle*, Walter Map, Mill on *Liberty*, Hooker's *Ecclesiastical Polity*, the *Annual Register*, Froissart, Adam Smith's *Wealth of Nations*, *Domesday Book*, *Le Morte d'Arthur*, Campbell's *Lives of the Lord Chancellors*, Boswell's *Johnson*, Barbour's *The Bruce*, Hakluyt's *Voyages*, Clarendon, Macaulay, the Plays of Shakespeare, Shelley's *Prometheus Unbound, The Faerie Queene*, Palgrave's *Golden Treasury*, Bacon's *Essays*, Swinburne's *Poems and Ballads*, Fitzgerald's *Omar Khayyam*, Wordsworth, Browning, *Sartor Resartus*, Burton's *Anatomy of Melancholy*, Burke's *Letters on a Regicide Peace*, Ossian, *Piers Plowman*, Burke's *Thoughts on the Present Discontents*, Quarles, Newman's *Apologia*, Donne's *Sermons*, Ruskin, Blake, *The Deserted Village, Manfred*, Blair's *Grave, The Complaint of Deor*, Halley's *Festus*, Thompson's *Hound of Heaven*.[1]

All this may seem far removed from the manual of theology or the handbook of ethics that we look for but such is the Bible as it has come to us from those "most ancient authorities." This is not to say it does not contain theology or ethics: there is in it more theology than our ablest divines

[1] Quiller-Couch, Sir Arthur, *On the Art of Reading* (New York: G. P. Putnam's Sons, 1921), pp. 165–166.

have yet discovered and there are here ethical insights not yet fully fathomed by mortal men. There is in it, too, much that we might judge to be irrelevant to the purpose of a divine revelation. But who are we that we should so judge? The Bible is rooted in life, and all the crude stuff we have referred to is the stuff of life out of which, and through which, comes the divine revelation. The revelation is something tied up with life itself and the experience of the individual and the history of the nation Israel are the channels through which that revelation came to us. Thus the Bible will be seen to be, or, if we prefer the phrase of the Westminster divines, to contain the Word of God. It contains also man's response to that word. The Bible may thus be called the record of a divine revelation and the human response to that revelation. It is the sphere of the divine encounter, and the sphere of that encounter is human life.

All this implies a more vital view of the Bible. So much of it heretofore we have passed by or judged irrelevant to life. The Bible has been to us a thing of shreds and patches, a few bright spots here and there but largely barren as the desert. Psalm 23, Isaiah 6, 40, 53, snippets from the Prophets, minor and major, selections from the Gospels like the Sermon on the Mount, the stories of the Good Samaritan and the Prodigal Son, portions of the Pauline Epistles, such as I Corinthians 13, and some of the glowing imagery of the Apocalypse made familiar through its use in the Burial Service—that, for most of us, represents our knowledge of the Bible. But that is not the Bible: that is to mistake the part for the whole. We must "survey all the land" if we would enter into the fulness of our noble heritage. When we thus view the Bible it is seen to be strangely relevant to life.

c) UNIVERSAL INFLUENCE

All our noblest literature bears the impress of this book and testifies to its vitalizing power. Milton, Shakespeare, Chaucer, Spenser echo its teaching while Dante delights in, and builds upon it. From Cowper to Wordsworth, from Coleridge to Tennyson, the Bible has been the *fons et origo* of all great poetic work. The art of Fra Angelico and Raphael, of Da Vinci, Rubens, and Rembrandt derives its inspiration and ideas from the same source. The music of Handel, Haydn, and Mendelssohn, of Palestrina and Bach has its origin here. Has not Bach's Passion Music been called the Fifth Gospel? The bold genius of Luther, the reforming zeal of John Knox, the glowing imagination of Bunyan, the spiritual passion of Whitefield—all find their roots in the Bible. The hundred best books, the hundred greatest pictures, the hundred noblest strains of music, all owe their being and continuing power to the Book of Books. Here indeed is a book of vivifying power: here is *the Book that is alive*.

l) THE PRESENT DISCONCERTING SITUATION

In view of all this the present situation in regard to the Bible is highly disconcerting. Statistics tell us that this book is the world's best-seller: it has been translated into more than a thousand tongues. But the Bible is not being read today. It has become *the Book that Nobody Knows*. There are elements of danger in the present situation and we should give serious thought to this matter.

In speaking of the Puritan period in England the historian John Richard Green makes this observation:

> England became the people of a book and that book was the Bible.[2]

[2] John R. Green, *A Short History of the English People*, Vol. II, p. 431 (*Everyman Edition*).

A people of the Book may not necessarily be a people of God and there were certainly many unlovely features in the character of the Puritans in old England and the Pilgrim Fathers of New England. But it is one of the ironies of history that by their attitudes and actions they made it difficult for their successors to continue as a people of the Book. The experience of persecution under an established church in England compelled the Pilgrim Fathers to a complete separation of Church and State. Doubtless there are great advantages in such an arrangement, but it may well be questioned whether we, the children of those fathers, have not passed beyond their real intention or the intention of the framers of the American Constitution. The recent decision by the Supreme Court whereby children may not be released during school hours for religious education accentuates the present evil situation. Reading, writing, and arithmetic will continue to be taught in our schools but religion has become something more and more remote from practical life. The "three R's" will appear as belonging to the core of education but religion will appear as something not as essential or wholly nonessential. This was certainly not the intention of the framers of our Constitution. At the moment it would appear that the idea that the State should be neutral as between churches is now giving place to the idea that the State should be neutral between all forms of religion on one side and an aggressive secularism on the other. The end of this thing is sure. Religious inspirations will cease to flow through the life of our communities and before long—if not already—we shall see our domestic institutions usurping the place of religious faith and functioning against religion. Doubtless we shall still point the finger of scorn at the Nazis and the Bolsheviks, but there will be small reason for this nationalistic pride

Our culture will be completely secularized and if the light in us be darkness how great will be that darkness.

The present writer has had experience of two national cultures and in some respects they are strangely diverse. Until twenty-three years ago he was a British subject, educated in Scottish schools and universities. In those schools the Bible was taught in the same way as reading, writing, and arithmetic. And the teaching was enforced with the same physical sanctions. The writer may claim to know the English Bible, the Authorized version, but that knowledge came to him mainly through the pores of his skin. It was beaten in with rods amid strong crying and tears. The Sunday School teaching may have been less rigorous but it was equally effective. In the home the Bible was read daily in family worship. And the author will not cease to give thanks for that training. In the theological school every student was examined in such a way that he had to have real knowledge of the text and letter of the Bible from Genesis to Revelation. The minister of the Church of Scotland might not know Hebrew and Greek to perfection—though they were not deficient in those respects—but he did know the Bible. The precise value of this educational procedure might be open to question but most observers are agreed in ascribing its forceful strength to this Bible foundation.

Recently, however, discerning spirits in Britain have become rather anxious about certain things. The Bible is no longer taught in the same fashion and corporal punishment is largely abolished. Such volumes as Sir Richard Livingstone's *Education for a World Adrift*[3] and H. G. Wood's *Christianity and Civilisation*[4] show the concern felt regarding the

---

[3]Sir Richard Livingstone, *Education for a World Adrift* (Current Problems No. 17) (1944). Cp. also *The Future of Education*. Do. (1945) (No. 6).

[4]H. G. Wood, *Christianity and Civilisation* (Current Problems No. 16) (1942).

decay of Bible reading and Bible teaching in Britain. As early as 1921 the *London Times Literary Supplement* of November tenth of that year called attention to the deteriorating situation in these words:

> It can be truly said that we are a people of books, even of many books, though perhaps no longer of one Book. In that last confession lies one of our present misfortunes, for nothing has, in the past, kept the nation together so closely, uniting all its members in a common language, common thought, and common culture, as our English Bible. . . . It was the common and immediately accessible source for the English people of a humanism different only in degree from that of the classics. As the practice of reading the Bible, regularly and religiously, at home has decreased, by so much has the nation deliberately impoverished itself.

These words are of high significance coming from such a source. Sir Richard Livingstone (President of Corpus Christi College, Oxford), who feels the pressure of this situation and refers to the present generation as "the Age without Standards," remarks:

> Lord Bryce was once asked: "What do you think would be the effect of the disappearance of religious education from the schools?" "I can't answer that," he replied, "till three generations have passed."[5]

Character grows slowly and deterioration is a gradual process. It would seem, however, as if the process were swifter than Lord Bryce thought. When the roots of a tree are cut it is only a matter of time until it finally withers and dies. In this connection Sir Richard aptly cites the words of Plato:

> It is not the life of knowledge, not even if it includes all the sciences, that creates happiness and wellbeing, but a

[5] Sir R. Livingstone, *op. cit.,* p. 11.

single branch of knowledge—the science of good and evil. If you exclude this from the other branches, medicine will be equally able to give us health, and shoemaking shoes, and weaving clothes. Seamanship will still save life at sea and strategy win battles. But without the knowledge of good and evil the use and excellence of these sciences will be found to have failed us.[6]

Science, economics, sociology, industry, and commerce have amply cared for our material needs: they have provided the frame of society, but that society is failing and falling at the moment for lack of "the knowledge of good and evil." The body politic is waxing fat and luxurious but the national soul is starved and emaciated.

Let us move nearer home and look at ourselves. The present writer has been training ministers for over twenty years and he has found few men training for the ministry who knew the Bible well. He has found many who seemed to have very little knowledge of what the Bible really is. We need say no more on that or tell tales out of school. Let us look again at the secular press. In *Time* magazine of September 25, 1950, we find this:

> What does the College generation actually know about the rudiments of the Hebrew-Christian tradition? To this question an article in the *Christian Century* last week answered: "It is almost illiterate."

The article goes on to give the experience of a teacher in various universities throughout the U. S. A. from Virginia to Texas. He tells us he examined more than two thousand students in both church and non-church colleges. More than half of them, he reported ruefully, spell "prophet" as "profit." That may be the straw that indicates the general direction

[6]Sir. R. Livingstone, *op. cit.*, p. 25. The words quoted are from Plato, Charmides 174.

of the wind in these parts. Almost all of these students had
a religious background but he goes on:

> In a typical group of 83 in a non-church college only three
> had no religious background. Of the others 68 were Prot-
> estants, eleven Roman Catholics and one Greek Orthodox.
> Yet only four of the 83 could list all the Ten Command-
> ments; 70 could not name the four Gospels; 74 could not
> describe "even approximately" what Jesus stressed as the
> two greatest commandments.

This may appear to have elements of comedy in it, but it
has too many elements of real tragedy to allow us even to
smile at it.

The situation, however, is not without hope, and the same
professor goes on to say:

> The student's image of God is vague. But his hunger and
> thirst after righteousness and the things of the Spirit are
> keen, even if confused. The Bible is a strange new Book of
> Life to him. When he has a chance to read it with self-
> criticism and with Christian guidance, he is fascinated with
> it and with its lasting insights and demands.

For the Bible springs from life and it ministers to life and
it finds us in the deepest parts of our being.

e) REASONS—AND A REMEDY

It may not be a simple matter to explain this whole situation. One might point to the growing secularization of
life. We live in a secular age and secularism just means
worldliness. Last century we had "other-worldliness" but that
has gone with the horse and buggy age. We live in a money
culture and a machine age; spiritual vision has given place
to sordid *Realpolitik* and far-seeing statesmen have been

replaced by puny politicians whose ears are to the ground and their eye on the main chance. Scientific progress and technological skills have far outrun our moral and spiritual attainments. There is a tremendous gap between our engineering triumphs and our ethical insights. We all have porcelain bathtubs in our homes, but we do not have the peace of God in our hearts. We know all about the thrill of speed on the open road, but what do we know of the rapture of the noble thought? The Bible that used to repose on the living room table has been displaced by the Sears Roebuck catalog. Things ride the man and it is little wonder that a book which condemns materialism and holds that man's life consists not "in the abundance of things which he possesseth" lies unheeded and unread. We have given too many hostages to time to think of the eternal.

Or again it may be that throughout the world today there is a spirit of revolt. Everywhere inherited traditions are being questioned: the faith of our fathers is eclipsed and in many cases completely repudiated. The spirit that denies is abroad in the world: old empires are falling apart and monarchs are being retired from business. Economic pressures and political events have brought it about that multitudes everywhere find difficulty in keeping body and soul together. Our whole civilization seems sick unto death and people turn in desperation to desperate remedies. They have ceased to believe "that there is balm in Gilead" or any physician there that will heal their mortal malady. Totalitarian philosophies and Communist doctrines find ready lodgment in the minds of people reduced to such extremities. The whole world is in revolt and great nations have repudiated Christianity.

Doubtless there is force in these considerations. But we wonder if there is not even greater force in another consideration. Have not we Protestants been guilty of the sin of Bibliolatry? Have we not worshipped the book as the Roman Catholic worships Mary and practises Mariolatry. About two million copies of the new Revised Standard Version have been sold; will they be read? Nobody likes to be found without a Bible in his home. Is it not just this fact that has led us to set the Bible on a pinnacle and place it out of relation to life, to common work-a-day life and worship? There will be real gain if we should begin to take it down from the pinnacle and set it back into common life from which it first sprang. In the present situation we cannot afford to keep it on a pinnacle out of daily use. Our only hope is in His Word.

Selected Bibliography

(other works cited in the text)

CHAPTERS 1 AND 2

ALBRIGHT, W. F., *The Archaeology of Palestine*: Pelican Books (A 199)

COOK, STANLEY, *An Introduction to the Bible*: Pelican Books (B 144)

DEANE, ANTHONY C., *How to Enjoy the Bible*, London: n. d.

DINSMORE, C. A., *The English Bible as Literature*, Cambridge (Mass.): 1931

HERDER, J. G. VON, *Vom Geist der hebräischen Poesie*, Dessau: 1782–83

MACFADYEN, J. E., *The Use of the Old Testament*, London: 1922

MANSON, T. W. (editor), *A Companion to the Bible*, New York: 1939

PEAKE, A. S., *The Bible, Its Origin, Significance, and Abiding Value*, London: 1913

JAMES, M. R., *The Apocryphal New Testament*, Oxford: 1924

CHAPTERS 3 AND 4

BEWER, J. A., *Literature of the Old Testament*, New York: 1944

CAIRNS, D. S., *The Riddle of the World*, London: 1937

ELMSLIE, W. A. L., *Studies in Life from Jewish Proverbs*, London: n. d.

OESTERLEY, W. O. E., *The Book of Proverbs*, New York: 1929

RANSTON, H., *The Old Testament Wisdom Books and their Teaching*, London: 1939

TRENCH, R. C., *Proverbs and their Lessons*, London: 1857

CHAPTERS 5, 6, 7, 9

DEVINE, M., *The Story of Job*, London: 1921

LINDBLOM, J., *La Composition du Livre de Job*, Lund: 1945

PEAKE, A. S., *Job* (Century Bible series), London: 1904

————, *The Problem of Suffering in the Old Testament*, London: 1904

ROBINSON, H. W., *The Cross of Job*, London: n. d.

————, *Suffering Human and Divine*, London: 1940

STEVENSON, W. B., *The Poem of Job*, (Schweich Lectures), Oxford: 1947

————, *Notes on the Poem of Job*, Aberdeen: 1951

STRAHAN, J., *The Book of Job*, Edinburgh: 1914 (2nd edition)

CHAPTER 8

BUDDE, K., *Die Heilige Schriften des Alten Testament* (edited by Kautzsch), London: 1923 (7th edition)

BURKITT, F. C., *Ecclesiastes rendered into English Verse*, London: 1922

CHEYNE, T. K., *Job and Solomon*, London: 1887

DEVINE, M., *Confessions of an Adventurous Soul*, London: 1916

GALLING, K., *Der Prediger* (*in Die fünf Megilloth, Handbuch zum A. T.*), Tübingen: 1940

GINSBURG, H. L., *Studies in Koheleth*, New York: 1950

GORDIS, R., *The Wisdom of Ecclesiastes*, New York: 1950

HERTZBERG, H. W., *Der Prediger* (*Qohelet*), *Kommentar zum A. T.*, Leipzig: 1932

MACDONALD, D. B., *The Hebrew Literary Genius*, Princeton: 1933

————, *The Hebrew Philosophical Genius*, Princeton: 1936

McNeile, A. H., *An Introduction to Ecclesiastes*, Cambridge: 1904

Pedersen, J., *Scepticisme Israélite*, Paris: 1931

Williams, A. L., *Ecclesiastes* (Cambridge Bible series), Cambridge: 1922 (The older edition by Dean Plumptre is very valuable for its appendices.)

CHAPTER 10

Livingstone, Sir R., *Education for a World Adrift*, Cambridge: 1944

————, *The Future in Education*, Cambridge: 1945

Simpson, H., *Altars of Earth*, London: 1928

Wood, H. G., *Christianity and Civilisation*, Cambridge: 1943

Index of Scripture References

Index of Names and Subjects